Empath
SURVIVAL JOURNAL

FOR AWAKENING YOUR EMPATH GIFTS AND RECHARGING YOUR ENERGY

KIMBERLY DAWN

Copyright © 2019 by Kimberly Dawn. All Right Reserved.

No part of this publication may be reproduced, distributed, or transmitted in any form or by any means, including photocopying, recording, or other electronic or mechanical methods, or by any information storage and retrieval system without the prior written permission of the publisher, except in the case of very brief quotations embodied in critical reviews and certain other noncommercial uses permitted by copyright law.

How To Know If You're An Empath?

Empaths feel everything more intensely because they experience the world through their highly tuned senses. They are intuitive whether they know it or not. Empaths are compassionate, heart-centered, keen listeners and have a sense of deep loyalty for those they love.

Empaths naturally put themselves in other people's shoes and easily understand your emotions because they feel the feelings of others deeply within. The downfall for empaths is they can end up being sponges for the negative energy of others and end up absorbing the negative emotions, thoughts, and even sickness from others due to their innate gifted ability to feel what others are feeling.

Absorbing the negative emotions and energy of others can supersede empaths from only taking in peaceful, positive love energy from the world. However, if empaths were around mostly peace filled, loving, calm energy all day they would do much better because the positive would help them grow in Divine light, inner strength and they'd be able to develop their empath gifts and abilities easier.

The negative emotions of others and the negativity of the world feel depleting, violating and exhausting making them easy targets for energy draining selfish people or emotional vampires.

Some empaths may gain weight because they subconsciously are trying to buffer themselves from other people's draining negative energy. Many empaths get overwhelmed in relationships and sometimes remain single from not learning how to navigate their enhanced sensitivities and cohabitation needs in a relationship.

As empaths knowingly or unknowingly absorb the stress and negativity energy from others, this can cause anxiety, depression, chronic fatigue, fibromyalgia, chronic pain, panic attacks, and food, sex or drug addiction.

This journal was created for you and all of my clients because I understand the needs of being an empath first hand because I am one.

My clients who are also empaths have shown me directly how uniquely valuable being an empath is in today's world because empaths have the compassion, care, deep understanding of human nature, but also their ability to nurture others with their emotional intelligence.

Being an empath doesn't have to make you sick or feel horrible all the time. Now that my clients and I know how to disconnect and clear other people's negative energy from our auric field, thoughts, and emotions we feel more centered, connected, calm, and peaceful daily.

I believe the world needs more empaths who are in-tuned, well balanced, and Divinely connected to their higher-selves (their soul). Balanced empaths would give non-sensitive humans more examples of how to be a compassionate, healthy, and stable human being.

Are You An Empath Quiz

- **Do you get drained by being in large crowds and need time alone to get rejuvenated again?**

- **Have you been called overly sensitive or too emotional?**

- **Do you get your feelings hurt easily?**

- **If a loved one or friend is stressed or going through a tough time, do you begin to feel this as well?**

- **Do you prefer to take your own form of transportation to events, places or locations so you can leave when you prefer?**

- **Do you overeat to cope with emotional stress or the negativity from the day?**

- **Are you afraid of losing yourself in a relationship or becoming overtaken by certain friendships?**

Answering yes to 3 or more questions shows you why you are an emotional empath.

Answering yes to 1-3 questions indicates you have some empathic tendencies and are partly an empath.

Recognizing and acknowledging you're an empath and that you have empath gifts and abilities is the first step learning how to disconnect and clear the negative energy of others from within and around you. Answering the questions in this journal will help you not get overwhelmed by the negative stress of others around you and be able to improve your health, well-being, and peace of mind more easily and effortlessly.

How You Can Find Balance As An Empath

- Practice these empath self-care strategies to recharge your energy.

- Allow peaceful quiet time to decompress emotionally and energetically each day.

- Reduce excessive stimulation of over-ingesting watching TV, reading social media, watching the news, or listening to others who drain you who you don't want to be talking to in the first place.

- Spend time in nature, taking walks or meditating on a rock or on earth to ground your energy with Mother Earth's healing power. Taking off your shoes if you can for a time and allowing yourself to let go of all the "have to's" for the time being.

- Meditate daily to unwind when you get overwhelmed and overloaded. You can do the FREE Archangel Michael Anxiety Relief Meditation found at ArchangelsBless.com.

- Say no to others who ask too much of you; it's not necessary to compromise yourself for the sake of pleasing others.

- If spending time with certain people drains you, set limits with the amount of time you socialize.

- Take your own vehicle or transportation if you know you want to leave certain events sooner than others.

- Eat highly nutritious whole foods before events, parties or while traveling to help yourself stay grounded, centered, and emotionally stable. Preplanning your eating is a good self-care practice because the more your blood sugar is stable by ingesting purer whole foods, the more your energy and auric field will become stronger each day you practice this.

- If you feel the urge to go on an unhealthy food binge, practice meditation for 5-15 minutes beforehand. Use the Free Anxiety Relief Archangel Michael Meditation found at ArchangelsBless.com to receive balancing, grounding energy. Using the Anxiety Relief Archangel Michael Meditation will help you discharge other people's negative energy out of your energy bodies, thoughts and emotions so that you steer yourself to healthier food choices that will further invigorate you with balanced tranquility.

- Be sure to have your own quiet space in your home environment so that you can connect directly to your higher-self and Divine light while you meditate. Having time to yourself in a peaceful environment helps you release the stress you've absorbed from others more quickly the more you do it.

What else would you like to add to this list that helps you when you become emotionally overloaded?

What else helps you feel safe and healthily release stress so that your natural empath gifts and abilities can blossom and flourish?

Brainstorm what else you know works for you below:

What are your Life Dreams and Goals (Big and Small)?

What do you most want? What haven't you been able to achieve yet that you'd like to accomplish, be, do or have? List everything you can think of:

Answering Your Journal Questions. Tips For Each Section:

How did you feel when you first woke up this morning?

Recall the overall emotion you felt when you first woke up. Noting your emotional state will help you gauge your feelings later.

How did you feel in your dreams last night?

Noting how you felt in your dreams will help you develop your empath gifts and abilities because you'll be directly connecting to your subconscious mind and your higher-self as you tap into your dream emotions.

What intuitive messages does your higher self (your soul) want you to know today?

Free-flow writing is best. Getting intuitive messages from your higher self, your soul is usually most natural to do first thing in the morning or right after you finish meditating and clearing your mind. Writing down any words that come to you helps you open up your empath gift of communicating with your higher-self because you are tapping into your soul's powerful healing energy as you do it.

What signs or symbols did you encounter or receive? What intuitive messages do you get through those signs or symbols you encountered?

Writing down any signs or symbols, you saw in your waking state or your dream state in your mind's eye or physically will help you note what each sign and symbol means for you. Play with this one; there are no right or wrong answers here.

Describe any people you encountered or circumstances that happened today that drained your energy:

Jotting down who drains your energy or what situations or people you encountered that caused you emotional stress will help you become more consciously aware of what you could do in the future to protect yourself emotionally, energetically, and spiritually.

How did you feel after this happened, what were your thoughts, and how was your body left feeling?

Your answers here assist you with becoming clear about how certain people, situations, or events affect you emotionally and energetically. When you make notes about the aftermath that you feel, you'll be developing your empath inner awareness and gifts about what exactly is going on energetically in that situation. You'll be surprised by what you insightfully realize.

What spiritual cleansing, energetic cord cutting, energy healing, chakra clearing, visualization, mantra, prayer or meditation method did you use to clear the residual energy afterward from your body and auric field?

Experimenting with what methods help you the best are crucial because you'll begin to see a beautiful pattern emerge. You'll be able to develop more tools in your empath toolbox that will reduce anxiety and bring you the peace of mind you so deserve.

what body sensations, intuitive thoughts or emotions did you feel today that helped you know you are going in the right direction for you?

Your confidence with your empathic gifts and intuitive abilities gets developed much more quickly when you consciously write down what body sensations, thoughts or emotions happen to you when you know you're on track or headed in the right direction for you. It's okay if this goes against the grain of what other people want from you.

what body sensations, intuitive thoughts or emotions did you feel today that helped you know you could be "off track" and need to take a step back?

Writing down anything that caused your gut to tighten up or made you feel energetically off-kilter will help you begin to intuitively unfold why some negative situations or people may not be the best thing for you.

what (pure) whole, nutritious foods did you eat that helped you feel better? Did you drink enough water? What foods did you eat that caused you to feel worse?

As an empath you may have more food sensitivities then you think you have. When you are aware of the specific foods and also the food combinations that cause you to feel lethargic, have allergic reactions, digestive problems, headaches or pain in your body you'll be able to choose foods that work better for you more easily.

How do you want tomorrow to be different?

What would help you feel even better about yourself tomorrow? It's about progress, not perfection. Making the smallest of improvements to your daily routine will bring you exponential results six months or 1 year from now. Exponential rewards await you as you take care of your well-being and make new choices that empower your life.

What tiny (baby) steps would you like to take tomorrow for improved health, self-care, and that will move your life dreams and goals forward?

Remember the smallest of action steps bring 10X rewards 1-2 years from now. Breaking your goals and tasks down into the tiniest of steps, i.e., research how to do something new, will help you take that micro step easier than looking at your life dreams as a huge milestone that seems unattainable. The smaller you chunk tasks down the more efficiently your brain will believe it can accomplish your vision.

Circle or shade in how you feel today with one of the three face icons.

What are you most proud of about yourself for today?

Pretend you're talking to a baby that you are watching over. What would you tell it from your heart that you know to be true?

Additional Tips:

You can go at your own pace; if you want to use this as a daily journal and use it every day in the beginning, middle or end of the day the choice is yours — do what suits your fancy!

You can choose to use this as a weekly or monthly journal. Either one is perfectly okay because as you pick up the journal, your internal navigational compass begins to help you right where you last left off.

Date   Day   Daily Intention
___   ___   ___

How did you feel when you first woke up this morning?

How did you feel in your dreams last night?

What intuitive messages does your higher self (your soul) want you to know today?

What signs or symbols did you encounter or receive? What intuitive messages do you get through those signs or symbols you encountered?

Describe any people you encountered or circumstances that happened today that drained your energy:

How did you feel after this happened, what were your thoughts, and how was your body left feeling?

What spiritual cleansing, energetic cord cutting, energy healing, chakra clearing, visualization, mantra, prayer or meditation method did you use to clear the residual energy afterward from your body and auric field?

- [ ] Spiritual Cleansing
- [ ] Energy Healing
- [ ] Mantras
- [ ] Meditation
- [ ] Other
- [ ] Energetic Cord Cutting
- [ ] Chakra Clearing
- [ ] Visualization
- [ ] Prayers

What body sensations, intuitive thoughts or emotions did you feel today that helped you know you are going in the right direction for you?

What body sensations, intuitive thoughts or emotions did you feel today that helped you know you could be "off track" and need to take a step back?

What (pure) whole, nutritious foods did you eat that helped you feel better? Did you drink enough water?

What foods did you eat that caused you to feel worse?

How do you want tomorrow to be different?

What tiny (baby) steps would you like to take tomorrow for improved health, self-care, and that will move your life dreams and goals forward?

Circle or shade in how you feel today with one of the three face icons:

What are you most proud of about yourself for today?

Notes, brainstorming ideas or doodles:

Date _____ Day _____ Daily Intention _____

How did you feel when you first woke up this morning?

How did you feel in your dreams last night?

What intuitive messages does your higher self (your soul) want you to know today?

What signs or symbols did you encounter or receive? What intuitive messages do you get through those signs or symbols you encountered?

Describe any people you encountered or circumstances that happened today that drained your energy:

How did you feel after this happened, what were your thoughts, and how was your body left feeling?

What spiritual cleansing, energetic cord cutting, energy healing, chakra clearing, visualization, mantra, prayer or meditation method did you use to clear the residual energy afterward from your body and auric field?

- [ ] Spiritual Cleansing
- [ ] Energy Healing
- [ ] Mantras
- [ ] Meditation
- [ ] Other
- [ ] Energetic Cord Cutting
- [ ] Chakra Clearing
- [ ] Visualization
- [ ] Prayers

What body sensations, intuitive thoughts or emotions did you feel today that helped you know you are going in the right direction for you?

What body sensations, intuitive thoughts or emotions did you feel today that helped you know you could be "off track" and need to take a step back?

What (pure) whole, nutritious foods did you eat that helped you feel better? Did you drink enough water?

what foods did you eat that caused you to feel worse?

How do you want tomorrow to be different?

what tiny (baby) steps would you like to take tomorrow for improved health, self-care, and that will move your life dreams and goals forward?

Circle or shade in how you feel today with one of the three face icons:

what are you most proud of about yourself for today?

Notes, brainstorming ideas or doodles:

Date	Day	Daily Intention
_____	_____	_____

How did you feel when you first woke up this morning?

How did you feel in your dreams last night?

What intuitive messages does your higher self (your soul) want you to know today?

What signs or symbols did you encounter or receive? What intuitive messages do you get through those signs or symbols you encountered?

Describe any people you encountered or circumstances that happened today that drained your energy:

How did you feel after this happened, what were your thoughts, and how was your body left feeling?

What spiritual cleansing, energetic cord cutting, energy healing, chakra clearing, visualization, mantra, prayer or meditation method did you use to clear the residual energy afterward from your body and auric field?

- [ ] Spiritual Cleansing
- [ ] Energy Healing
- [ ] Mantras
- [ ] Meditation
- [ ] Other
- [ ] Energetic Cord Cutting
- [ ] Chakra Clearing
- [ ] Visualization
- [ ] Prayers

What body sensations, intuitive thoughts or emotions did you feel today that helped you know you are going in the right direction for you?

What body sensations, intuitive thoughts or emotions did you feel today that helped you know you could be "off track" and need to take a step back?

What (pure) whole, nutritious foods did you eat that helped you feel better? Did you drink enough water?

What foods did you eat that caused you to feel worse?

How do you want tomorrow to be different?

What tiny (baby) steps would you like to take tomorrow for improved health, self-care, and that will move your life dreams and goals forward?

Circle or shade in how you feel today with one of the three face icons:

What are you most proud of about yourself for today?

Notes, brainstorming ideas or doodles:

Date _____   Day _____   Daily Intention _____

How did you feel when you first woke up this morning?

How did you feel in your dreams last night?

What intuitive messages does your higher self (your soul) want you to know today?

What signs or symbols did you encounter or receive? What intuitive messages do you get through those signs or symbols you encountered?

Describe any people you encountered or circumstances that happened today that drained your energy:

How did you feel after this happened, what were your thoughts, and how was your body left feeling?

What spiritual cleansing, energetic cord cutting, energy healing, chakra clearing, visualization, mantra, prayer or meditation method did you use to clear the residual energy afterward from your body and auric field?

- ☐ Spiritual Cleansing
- ☐ Energy Healing
- ☐ Mantras
- ☐ Meditation
- ☐ Other
- ☐ Energetic Cord Cutting
- ☐ Chakra Clearing
- ☐ Visualization
- ☐ Prayers

What body sensations, intuitive thoughts or emotions did you feel today that helped you know you are going in the right direction for you?

What body sensations, intuitive thoughts or emotions did you feel today that helped you know you could be "off track" and need to take a step back?

What (pure) whole, nutritious foods did you eat that helped you feel better? Did you drink enough water?

what foods did you eat that caused you to feel worse?

How do you want tomorrow to be different?

what tiny (baby) steps would you like to take tomorrow for improved health, self-care, and that will move your life dreams and goals forward?

Circle or shade in how you feel today with one of the three face icons:

what are you most proud of about yourself for today?

Notes, brainstorming ideas or doodles:

Date _____ Day _____ Daily Intention _____

How did you feel when you first woke up this morning?

How did you feel in your dreams last night?

What intuitive messages does your higher self (your soul) want you to know today?

What signs or symbols did you encounter or receive? What intuitive messages do you get through those signs or symbols you encountered?

Describe any people you encountered or circumstances that happened today that drained your energy:

How did you feel after this happened, what were your thoughts, and how was your body left feeling?

What spiritual cleansing, energetic cord cutting, energy healing, chakra clearing, visualization, mantra, prayer or meditation method did you use to clear the residual energy afterward from your body and auric field?

- [ ] Spiritual Cleansing
- [ ] Energy Healing
- [ ] Mantras
- [ ] Meditation
- [ ] Other
- [ ] Energetic Cord Cutting
- [ ] Chakra Clearing
- [ ] Visualization
- [ ] Prayers

What body sensations, intuitive thoughts or emotions did you feel today that helped you know you are going in the right direction for you?

What body sensations, intuitive thoughts or emotions did you feel today that helped you know you could be "off track" and need to take a step back?

What (pure) whole, nutritious foods did you eat that helped you feel better? Did you drink enough water?

What foods did you eat that caused you to feel worse?

How do you want tomorrow to be different?

What tiny (baby) steps would you like to take tomorrow for improved health, self-care, and that will move your life dreams and goals forward?

Circle or shade in how you feel today with one of the three face icons:

What are you most proud of about yourself for today?

Notes, brainstorming ideas or doodles:

Date _____   Day _____   Daily Intention _____

How did you feel when you first woke up this morning?

How did you feel in your dreams last night?

What intuitive messages does your higher self (your soul) want you to know today?

What signs or symbols did you encounter or receive? What intuitive messages do you get through those signs or symbols you encountered?

Describe any people you encountered or circumstances that happened today that drained your energy:

How did you feel after this happened, what were your thoughts, and how was your body left feeling?

What spiritual cleansing, energetic cord cutting, energy healing, chakra clearing, visualization, mantra, prayer or meditation method did you use to clear the residual energy afterward from your body and auric field?

- [ ] Spiritual Cleansing
- [ ] Energy Healing
- [ ] Mantras
- [ ] Meditation
- [ ] Other
- [ ] Energetic Cord Cutting
- [ ] Chakra Clearing
- [ ] Visualization
- [ ] Prayers

What body sensations, intuitive thoughts or emotions did you feel today that helped you know you are going in the right direction for you?

What body sensations, intuitive thoughts or emotions did you feel today that helped you know you could be "off track" and need to take a step back?

What (pure) whole, nutritious foods did you eat that helped you feel better? Did you drink enough water?

what foods did you eat that caused you to feel worse?

How do you want tomorrow to be different?

what tiny (baby) steps would you like to take tomorrow for improved health, self-care, and that will move your life dreams and goals forward?

Circle or shade in how you feel today with one of the three face icons:

what are you most proud of about yourself for today?

Notes, brainstorming ideas or doodles:

Date   Day   Daily Intention

How did you feel when you first woke up this morning?

How did you feel in your dreams last night?

What intuitive messages does your higher self (your soul) want you to know today?

What signs or symbols did you encounter or receive? What intuitive messages do you get through those signs or symbols you encountered?

Describe any people you encountered or circumstances that happened today that drained your energy:

How did you feel after this happened, what were your thoughts, and how was your body left feeling?

What spiritual cleansing, energetic cord cutting, energy healing, chakra clearing, visualization, mantra, prayer or meditation method did you use to clear the residual energy afterward from your body and auric field?

- [ ] Spiritual Cleansing
- [ ] Energy Healing
- [ ] Mantras
- [ ] Meditation
- [ ] Other
- [ ] Energetic Cord Cutting
- [ ] Chakra Clearing
- [ ] Visualization
- [ ] Prayers

What body sensations, intuitive thoughts or emotions did you feel today that helped you know you are going in the right direction for you?

What body sensations, intuitive thoughts or emotions did you feel today that helped you know you could be "off track" and need to take a step back?

What (pure) whole, nutritious foods did you eat that helped you feel better? Did you drink enough water?

What foods did you eat that caused you to feel worse?

How do you want tomorrow to be different?

What tiny (baby) steps would you like to take tomorrow for improved health, self-care, and that will move your life dreams and goals forward?

Circle or shade in how you feel today with one of the three face icons:

What are you most proud of about yourself for today?

Notes, brainstorming ideas or doodles:

Date _____   Day _____   Daily Intention _____

How did you feel when you first woke up this morning?

How did you feel in your dreams last night?

What intuitive messages does your higher self (your soul) want you to know today?

What signs or symbols did you encounter or receive? What intuitive messages do you get through those signs or symbols you encountered?

Describe any people you encountered or circumstances that happened today that drained your energy:

How did you feel after this happened, what were your thoughts, and how was your body left feeling?

What spiritual cleansing, energetic cord cutting, energy healing, chakra clearing, visualization, mantra, prayer or meditation method did you use to clear the residual energy afterward from your body and auric field?

- [ ] Spiritual Cleansing
- [ ] Energy Healing
- [ ] Mantras
- [ ] Meditation
- [ ] Other
- [ ] Energetic Cord Cutting
- [ ] Chakra Clearing
- [ ] Visualization
- [ ] Prayers

What body sensations, intuitive thoughts or emotions did you feel today that helped you know you are going in the right direction for you?

What body sensations, intuitive thoughts or emotions did you feel today that helped you know you could be "off track" and need to take a step back?

What (pure) whole, nutritious foods did you eat that helped you feel better? Did you drink enough water?

What foods did you eat that caused you to feel worse?

How do you want tomorrow to be different?

What tiny (baby) steps would you like to take tomorrow for improved health, self-care, and that will move your life dreams and goals forward?

Circle or shade in how you feel today with one of the three face icons:

What are you most proud of about yourself for today?

Notes, brainstorming ideas or doodles:

Date _____ Day _____ Daily Intention _____

How did you feel when you first woke up this morning?

How did you feel in your dreams last night?

What intuitive messages does your higher self (your soul) want you to know today?

What signs or symbols did you encounter or receive? What intuitive messages do you get through those signs or symbols you encountered?

Describe any people you encountered or circumstances that happened today that drained your energy:

How did you feel after this happened, what were your thoughts, and how was your body left feeling?

What spiritual cleansing, energetic cord cutting, energy healing, chakra clearing, visualization, mantra, prayer or meditation method did you use to clear the residual energy afterward from your body and auric field?

- [ ] Spiritual Cleansing
- [ ] Energy Healing
- [ ] Mantras
- [ ] Meditation
- [ ] Other
- [ ] Energetic Cord Cutting
- [ ] Chakra Clearing
- [ ] Visualization
- [ ] Prayers

What body sensations, intuitive thoughts or emotions did you feel today that helped you know you are going in the right direction for you?

What body sensations, intuitive thoughts or emotions did you feel today that helped you know you could be "off track" and need to take a step back?

What (pure) whole, nutritious foods did you eat that helped you feel better? Did you drink enough water?

What foods did you eat that caused you to feel worse?

How do you want tomorrow to be different?

What tiny (baby) steps would you like to take tomorrow for improved health, self-care, and that will move your life dreams and goals forward?

Circle or shade in how you feel today with one of the three face icons:

What are you most proud of about yourself for today?

Notes, brainstorming ideas or doodles:

Date _____ Day _____ Daily Intention _____

How did you feel when you first woke up this morning?

How did you feel in your dreams last night?

What intuitive messages does your higher self (your soul) want you to know today?

What signs or symbols did you encounter or receive? What intuitive messages do you get through those signs or symbols you encountered?

Describe any people you encountered or circumstances that happened today that drained your energy:

How did you feel after this happened, what were your thoughts, and how was your body left feeling?

What spiritual cleansing, energetic cord cutting, energy healing, chakra clearing, visualization, mantra, prayer or meditation method did you use to clear the residual energy afterward from your body and auric field?

- [ ] Spiritual Cleansing
- [ ] Energy Healing
- [ ] Mantras
- [ ] Meditation
- [ ] Other
- [ ] Energetic Cord Cutting
- [ ] Chakra Clearing
- [ ] Visualization
- [ ] Prayers

What body sensations, intuitive thoughts or emotions did you feel today that helped you know you are going in the right direction for you?

What body sensations, intuitive thoughts or emotions did you feel today that helped you know you could be "off track" and need to take a step back?

What (pure) whole, nutritious foods did you eat that helped you feel better? Did you drink enough water?

What foods did you eat that caused you to feel worse?

How do you want tomorrow to be different?

What tiny (baby) steps would you like to take tomorrow for improved health, self-care, and that will move your life dreams and goals forward?

Circle or shade in how you feel today with one of the three face icons:

What are you most proud of about yourself for today?

Notes, brainstorming ideas or doodles:

Date _____ Day _____ Daily Intention _____

How did you feel when you first woke up this morning?

How did you feel in your dreams last night?

What intuitive messages does your higher self (your soul) want you to know today?

What signs or symbols did you encounter or receive? What intuitive messages do you get through those signs or symbols you encountered?

Describe any people you encountered or circumstances that happened today that drained your energy:

How did you feel after this happened, what were your thoughts, and how was your body left feeling?

What spiritual cleansing, energetic cord cutting, energy healing, chakra clearing, visualization, mantra, prayer or meditation method did you use to clear the residual energy afterward from your body and auric field?

- [ ] Spiritual Cleansing
- [ ] Energy Healing
- [ ] Mantras
- [ ] Meditation
- [ ] Other
- [ ] Energetic Cord Cutting
- [ ] Chakra Clearing
- [ ] Visualization
- [ ] Prayers

What body sensations, intuitive thoughts or emotions did you feel today that helped you know you are going in the right direction for you?

What body sensations, intuitive thoughts or emotions did you feel today that helped you know you could be "off track" and need to take a step back?

What (pure) whole, nutritious foods did you eat that helped you feel better? Did you drink enough water?

What foods did you eat that caused you to feel worse?

How do you want tomorrow to be different?

What tiny (baby) steps would you like to take tomorrow for improved health, self-care, and that will move your life dreams and goals forward?

Circle or shade in how you feel today with one of the three face icons:

What are you most proud of about yourself for today?

Notes, brainstorming ideas or doodles:

Date _____   Day _____   Daily Intention _____

How did you feel when you first woke up this morning?

How did you feel in your dreams last night?

What intuitive messages does your higher self (your soul) want you to know today?

What signs or symbols did you encounter or receive? What intuitive messages do you get through those signs or symbols you encountered?

Describe any people you encountered or circumstances that happened today that drained your energy:

How did you feel after this happened, what were your thoughts, and how was your body left feeling?

What spiritual cleansing, energetic cord cutting, energy healing, chakra clearing, visualization, mantra, prayer or meditation method did you use to clear the residual energy afterward from your body and auric field?

- [ ] Spiritual Cleansing
- [ ] Energy Healing
- [ ] Mantras
- [ ] Meditation
- [ ] Other
- [ ] Energetic Cord Cutting
- [ ] Chakra Clearing
- [ ] Visualization
- [ ] Prayers

What body sensations, intuitive thoughts or emotions did you feel today that helped you know you are going in the right direction for you?

What body sensations, intuitive thoughts or emotions did you feel today that helped you know you could be "off track" and need to take a step back?

What (pure) whole, nutritious foods did you eat that helped you feel better? Did you drink enough water?

What foods did you eat that caused you to feel worse?

How do you want tomorrow to be different?

What tiny (baby) steps would you like to take tomorrow for improved health, self-care, and that will move your life dreams and goals forward?

Circle or shade in how you feel today with one of the three face icons:

What are you most proud of about yourself for today?

Notes, brainstorming ideas or doodles:

Date	Day	Daily Intention

How did you feel when you first woke up this morning?

How did you feel in your dreams last night?

What intuitive messages does your higher self (your soul) want you to know today?

What signs or symbols did you encounter or receive? What intuitive messages do you get through those signs or symbols you encountered?

Describe any people you encountered or circumstances that happened today that drained your energy:

How did you feel after this happened, what were your thoughts, and how was your body left feeling?

What spiritual cleansing, energetic cord cutting, energy healing, chakra clearing, visualization, mantra, prayer or meditation method did you use to clear the residual energy afterward from your body and auric field?

- [ ] Spiritual Cleansing
- [ ] Energy Healing
- [ ] Mantras
- [ ] Meditation
- [ ] Other
- [ ] Energetic Cord Cutting
- [ ] Chakra Clearing
- [ ] Visualization
- [ ] Prayers

What body sensations, intuitive thoughts or emotions did you feel today that helped you know you are going in the right direction for you?

What body sensations, intuitive thoughts or emotions did you feel today that helped you know you could be "off track" and need to take a step back?

What (pure) whole, nutritious foods did you eat that helped you feel better? Did you drink enough water?

What foods did you eat that caused you to feel worse?

How do you want tomorrow to be different?

What tiny (baby) steps would you like to take tomorrow for improved health, self-care, and that will move your life dreams and goals forward?

Circle or shade in how you feel today with one of the three face icons:

What are you most proud of about yourself for today?

Notes, brainstorming ideas or doodles:

Date   Day   Daily Intention
_____   _____   _____

How did you feel when you first woke up this morning?

How did you feel in your dreams last night?

What intuitive messages does your higher self (your soul) want you to know today?

What signs or symbols did you encounter or receive? What intuitive messages do you get through those signs or symbols you encountered?

Describe any people you encountered or circumstances that happened today that drained your energy:

How did you feel after this happened, what were your thoughts, and how was your body left feeling?

What spiritual cleansing, energetic cord cutting, energy healing, chakra clearing, visualization, mantra, prayer or meditation method did you use to clear the residual energy afterward from your body and auric field?

- [ ] Spiritual Cleansing
- [ ] Energy Healing
- [ ] Mantras
- [ ] Meditation
- [ ] Other
- [ ] Energetic Cord Cutting
- [ ] Chakra Clearing
- [ ] Visualization
- [ ] Prayers

What body sensations, intuitive thoughts or emotions did you feel today that helped you know you are going in the right direction for you?

What body sensations, intuitive thoughts or emotions did you feel today that helped you know you could be "off track" and need to take a step back?

What (pure) whole, nutritious foods did you eat that helped you feel better? Did you drink enough water?

What foods did you eat that caused you to feel worse?

How do you want tomorrow to be different?

What tiny (baby) steps would you like to take tomorrow for improved health, self-care, and that will move your life dreams and goals forward?

Circle or shade in how you feel today with one of the three face icons:

What are you most proud of about yourself for today?

Notes, brainstorming ideas or doodles:

Date	Day	Daily Intention

How did you feel when you first woke up this morning?

How did you feel in your dreams last night?

What intuitive messages does your higher self (your soul) want you to know today?

What signs or symbols did you encounter or receive? What intuitive messages do you get through those signs or symbols you encountered?

Describe any people you encountered or circumstances that happened today that drained your energy:

How did you feel after this happened, what were your thoughts, and how was your body left feeling?

What spiritual cleansing, energetic cord cutting, energy healing, chakra clearing, visualization, mantra, prayer or meditation method did you use to clear the residual energy afterward from your body and auric field?

- [ ] Spiritual Cleansing
- [ ] Energy Healing
- [ ] Mantras
- [ ] Meditation
- [ ] Other
- [ ] Energetic Cord Cutting
- [ ] Chakra Clearing
- [ ] Visualization
- [ ] Prayers

What body sensations, intuitive thoughts or emotions did you feel today that helped you know you are going in the right direction for you?

What body sensations, intuitive thoughts or emotions did you feel today that helped you know you could be "off track" and need to take a step back?

What (pure) whole, nutritious foods did you eat that helped you feel better? Did you drink enough water?

What foods did you eat that caused you to feel worse?

How do you want tomorrow to be different?

What tiny (baby) steps would you like to take tomorrow for improved health, self-care, and that will move your life dreams and goals forward?

Circle or shade in how you feel today with one of the three face icons:

What are you most proud of about yourself for today?

Notes, brainstorming ideas or doodles:

Date _____   Day _____   Daily Intention _____

How did you feel when you first woke up this morning?

How did you feel in your dreams last night?

What intuitive messages does your higher self (your soul) want you to know today?

What signs or symbols did you encounter or receive? What intuitive messages do you get through those signs or symbols you encountered?

Describe any people you encountered or circumstances that happened today that drained your energy:

How did you feel after this happened, what were your thoughts, and how was your body left feeling?

What spiritual cleansing, energetic cord cutting, energy healing, chakra clearing, visualization, mantra, prayer or meditation method did you use to clear the residual energy afterward from your body and auric field?

- [ ] Spiritual Cleansing
- [ ] Energy Healing
- [ ] Mantras
- [ ] Meditation
- [ ] Other
- [ ] Energetic Cord Cutting
- [ ] Chakra Clearing
- [ ] Visualization
- [ ] Prayers

What body sensations, intuitive thoughts or emotions did you feel today that helped you know you are going in the right direction for you?

What body sensations, intuitive thoughts or emotions did you feel today that helped you know you could be "off track" and need to take a step back?

What (pure) whole, nutritious foods did you eat that helped you feel better? Did you drink enough water?

What foods did you eat that caused you to feel worse?

How do you want tomorrow to be different?

What tiny (baby) steps would you like to take tomorrow for improved health, self-care, and that will move your life dreams and goals forward?

Circle or shade in how you feel today with one of the three face icons:

What are you most proud of about yourself for today?

Notes, brainstorming ideas or doodles:

Date _____   Day _____   Daily Intention _____

How did you feel when you first woke up this morning?

How did you feel in your dreams last night?

What intuitive messages does your higher self (your soul) want you to know today?

What signs or symbols did you encounter or receive? What intuitive messages do you get through those signs or symbols you encountered?

Describe any people you encountered or circumstances that happened today that drained your energy:

How did you feel after this happened, what were your thoughts, and how was your body left feeling?

What spiritual cleansing, energetic cord cutting, energy healing, chakra clearing, visualization, mantra, prayer or meditation method did you use to clear the residual energy afterward from your body and auric field?

- [ ] Spiritual Cleansing
- [ ] Energy Healing
- [ ] Mantras
- [ ] Meditation
- [ ] Other
- [ ] Energetic Cord Cutting
- [ ] Chakra Clearing
- [ ] Visualization
- [ ] Prayers

What body sensations, intuitive thoughts or emotions did you feel today that helped you know you are going in the right direction for you?

What body sensations, intuitive thoughts or emotions did you feel today that helped you know you could be "off track" and need to take a step back?

What (pure) whole, nutritious foods did you eat that helped you feel better? Did you drink enough water?

What foods did you eat that caused you to feel worse?

How do you want tomorrow to be different?

What tiny (baby) steps would you like to take tomorrow for improved health, self-care, and that will move your life dreams and goals forward?

Circle or shade in how you feel today with one of the three face icons:

What are you most proud of about yourself for today?

Notes, brainstorming ideas or doodles:

Date _____   Day _____   Daily Intention _____

How did you feel when you first woke up this morning?

How did you feel in your dreams last night?

What intuitive messages does your higher self (your soul) want you to know today?

What signs or symbols did you encounter or receive? What intuitive messages do you get through those signs or symbols you encountered?

Describe any people you encountered or circumstances that happened today that drained your energy:

How did you feel after this happened, what were your thoughts, and how was your body left feeling?

What spiritual cleansing, energetic cord cutting, energy healing, chakra clearing, visualization, mantra, prayer or meditation method did you use to clear the residual energy afterward from your body and auric field?

- [ ] Spiritual Cleansing
- [ ] Energy Healing
- [ ] Mantras
- [ ] Meditation
- [ ] Other
- [ ] Energetic Cord Cutting
- [ ] Chakra Clearing
- [ ] Visualization
- [ ] Prayers

What body sensations, intuitive thoughts or emotions did you feel today that helped you know you are going in the right direction for you?

What body sensations, intuitive thoughts or emotions did you feel today that helped you know you could be "off track" and need to take a step back?

What (pure) whole, nutritious foods did you eat that helped you feel better? Did you drink enough water?

what foods did you eat that caused you to feel worse?

How do you want tomorrow to be different?

what tiny (baby) steps would you like to take tomorrow for improved health, self-care, and that will move your life dreams and goals forward?

Circle or shade in how you feel today with one of the three face icons:

What are you most proud of about yourself for today?

Notes, brainstorming ideas or doodles:

Date _____   Day _____   Daily Intention _____

How did you feel when you first woke up this morning?

How did you feel in your dreams last night?

What intuitive messages does your higher self (your soul) want you to know today?

What signs or symbols did you encounter or receive? What intuitive messages do you get through those signs or symbols you encountered?

Describe any people you encountered or circumstances that happened today that drained your energy:

How did you feel after this happened, what were your thoughts, and how was your body left feeling?

What spiritual cleansing, energetic cord cutting, energy healing, chakra clearing, visualization, mantra, prayer or meditation method did you use to clear the residual energy afterward from your body and auric field?

- [ ] Spiritual Cleansing
- [ ] Energy Healing
- [ ] Mantras
- [ ] Meditation
- [ ] Other
- [ ] Energetic Cord Cutting
- [ ] Chakra Clearing
- [ ] Visualization
- [ ] Prayers

What body sensations, intuitive thoughts or emotions did you feel today that helped you know you are going in the right direction for you?

What body sensations, intuitive thoughts or emotions did you feel today that helped you know you could be "off track" and need to take a step back?

What (pure) whole, nutritious foods did you eat that helped you feel better? Did you drink enough water?

What foods did you eat that caused you to feel worse?

How do you want tomorrow to be different?

What tiny (baby) steps would you like to take tomorrow for improved health, self-care, and that will move your life dreams and goals forward?

Circle or shade in how you feel today with one of the three face icons:

What are you most proud of about yourself for today?

Notes, brainstorming ideas or doodles:

Date _____ Day _____ Daily Intention _____

How did you feel when you first woke up this morning?

How did you feel in your dreams last night?

What intuitive messages does your higher self (your soul) want you to know today?

What signs or symbols did you encounter or receive? What intuitive messages do you get through those signs or symbols you encountered?

Describe any people you encountered or circumstances that happened today that drained your energy:

How did you feel after this happened, what were your thoughts, and how was your body left feeling?

What spiritual cleansing, energetic cord cutting, energy healing, chakra clearing, visualization, mantra, prayer or meditation method did you use to clear the residual energy afterward from your body and auric field?

- [ ] Spiritual Cleansing
- [ ] Energy Healing
- [ ] Mantras
- [ ] Meditation
- [ ] Other
- [ ] Energetic Cord Cutting
- [ ] Chakra Clearing
- [ ] Visualization
- [ ] Prayers

What body sensations, intuitive thoughts or emotions did you feel today that helped you know you are going in the right direction for you?

What body sensations, intuitive thoughts or emotions did you feel today that helped you know you could be "off track" and need to take a step back?

What (pure) whole, nutritious foods did you eat that helped you feel better? Did you drink enough water?

What foods did you eat that caused you to feel worse?

How do you want tomorrow to be different?

What tiny (baby) steps would you like to take tomorrow for improved health, self-care, and that will move your life dreams and goals forward?

Circle or shade in how you feel today with one of the three face icons:

What are you most proud of about yourself for today?

Notes, brainstorming ideas or doodles:

Date _____   Day _____   Daily Intention _____

How did you feel when you first woke up this morning?

How did you feel in your dreams last night?

What intuitive messages does your higher self (your soul) want you to know today?

What signs or symbols did you encounter or receive? What intuitive messages do you get through those signs or symbols you encountered?

Describe any people you encountered or circumstances that happened today that drained your energy:

How did you feel after this happened, what were your thoughts, and how was your body left feeling?

What spiritual cleansing, energetic cord cutting, energy healing, chakra clearing, visualization, mantra, prayer or meditation method did you use to clear the residual energy afterward from your body and auric field?

- [ ] Spiritual Cleansing
- [ ] Energy Healing
- [ ] Mantras
- [ ] Meditation
- [ ] Other
- [ ] Energetic Cord Cutting
- [ ] Chakra Clearing
- [ ] Visualization
- [ ] Prayers

What body sensations, intuitive thoughts or emotions did you feel today that helped you know you are going in the right direction for you?

What body sensations, intuitive thoughts or emotions did you feel today that helped you know you could be "off track" and need to take a step back?

What (pure) whole, nutritious foods did you eat that helped you feel better? Did you drink enough water?

What foods did you eat that caused you to feel worse?

How do you want tomorrow to be different?

What tiny (baby) steps would you like to take tomorrow for improved health, self-care, and that will move your life dreams and goals forward?

Circle or shade in how you feel today with one of the three face icons:

What are you most proud of about yourself for today?

Notes, brainstorming ideas or doodles:

Date _____ Day _____ Daily Intention _____

How did you feel when you first woke up this morning?

How did you feel in your dreams last night?

What intuitive messages does your higher self (your soul) want you to know today?

What signs or symbols did you encounter or receive? What intuitive messages do you get through those signs or symbols you encountered?

Describe any people you encountered or circumstances that happened today that drained your energy:

How did you feel after this happened, what were your thoughts, and how was your body left feeling?

What spiritual cleansing, energetic cord cutting, energy healing, chakra clearing, visualization, mantra, prayer or meditation method did you use to clear the residual energy afterward from your body and auric field?

- [ ] Spiritual Cleansing
- [ ] Energy Healing
- [ ] Mantras
- [ ] Meditation
- [ ] Other
- [ ] Energetic Cord Cutting
- [ ] Chakra Clearing
- [ ] Visualization
- [ ] Prayers

What body sensations, intuitive thoughts or emotions did you feel today that helped you know you are going in the right direction for you?

What body sensations, intuitive thoughts or emotions did you feel today that helped you know you could be "off track" and need to take a step back?

What (pure) whole, nutritious foods did you eat that helped you feel better? Did you drink enough water?

What foods did you eat that caused you to feel worse?

How do you want tomorrow to be different?

What tiny (baby) steps would you like to take tomorrow for improved health, self-care, and that will move your life dreams and goals forward?

Circle or shade in how you feel today with one of the three face icons:

What are you most proud of about yourself for today?

Notes, brainstorming ideas or doodles:

Date _____ Day _____ Daily Intention _____

How did you feel when you first woke up this morning?

How did you feel in your dreams last night?

What intuitive messages does your higher self (your soul) want you to know today?

What signs or symbols did you encounter or receive? What intuitive messages do you get through those signs or symbols you encountered?

Describe any people you encountered or circumstances that happened today that drained your energy:

How did you feel after this happened, what were your thoughts, and how was your body left feeling?

What spiritual cleansing, energetic cord cutting, energy healing, chakra clearing, visualization, mantra, prayer or meditation method did you use to clear the residual energy afterward from your body and auric field?

- [ ] Spiritual Cleansing
- [ ] Energy Healing
- [ ] Mantras
- [ ] Meditation
- [ ] Other
- [ ] Energetic Cord Cutting
- [ ] Chakra Clearing
- [ ] Visualization
- [ ] Prayers

What body sensations, intuitive thoughts or emotions did you feel today that helped you know you are going in the right direction for you?

What body sensations, intuitive thoughts or emotions did you feel today that helped you know you could be "off track" and need to take a step back?

What (pure) whole, nutritious foods did you eat that helped you feel better? Did you drink enough water?

What foods did you eat that caused you to feel worse?

How do you want tomorrow to be different?

What tiny (baby) steps would you like to take tomorrow for improved health, self-care, and that will move your life dreams and goals forward?

Circle or shade in how you feel today with one of the three face icons:

What are you most proud of about yourself for today?

Notes, brainstorming ideas or doodles:

Date	Day	Daily Intention

How did you feel when you first woke up this morning?

How did you feel in your dreams last night?

What intuitive messages does your higher self (your soul) want you to know today?

What signs or symbols did you encounter or receive? What intuitive messages do you get through those signs or symbols you encountered?

Describe any people you encountered or circumstances that happened today that drained your energy:

How did you feel after this happened, what were your thoughts, and how was your body left feeling?

What spiritual cleansing, energetic cord cutting, energy healing, chakra clearing, visualization, mantra, prayer or meditation method did you use to clear the residual energy afterward from your body and auric field?

- [ ] Spiritual Cleansing
- [ ] Energy Healing
- [ ] Mantras
- [ ] Meditation
- [ ] Other
- [ ] Energetic Cord Cutting
- [ ] Chakra Clearing
- [ ] Visualization
- [ ] Prayers

What body sensations, intuitive thoughts or emotions did you feel today that helped you know you are going in the right direction for you?

What body sensations, intuitive thoughts or emotions did you feel today that helped you know you could be "off track" and need to take a step back?

What (pure) whole, nutritious foods did you eat that helped you feel better? Did you drink enough water?

What foods did you eat that caused you to feel worse?

How do you want tomorrow to be different?

What tiny (baby) steps would you like to take tomorrow for improved health, self-care, and that will move your life dreams and goals forward?

Circle or shade in how you feel today with one of the three face icons:

What are you most proud of about yourself for today?

Notes, brainstorming ideas or doodles:

Date _____ Day _____ Daily Intention _____

How did you feel when you first woke up this morning?

How did you feel in your dreams last night?

What intuitive messages does your higher self (your soul) want you to know today?

What signs or symbols did you encounter or receive? What intuitive messages do you get through those signs or symbols you encountered?

Describe any people you encountered or circumstances that happened today that drained your energy:

How did you feel after this happened, what were your thoughts, and how was your body left feeling?

What spiritual cleansing, energetic cord cutting, energy healing, chakra clearing, visualization, mantra, prayer or meditation method did you use to clear the residual energy afterward from your body and auric field?

- [ ] Spiritual Cleansing
- [ ] Energy Healing
- [ ] Mantras
- [ ] Meditation
- [ ] Other
- [ ] Energetic Cord Cutting
- [ ] Chakra Clearing
- [ ] Visualization
- [ ] Prayers

What body sensations, intuitive thoughts or emotions did you feel today that helped you know you are going in the right direction for you?

What body sensations, intuitive thoughts or emotions did you feel today that helped you know you could be "off track" and need to take a step back?

What (pure) whole, nutritious foods did you eat that helped you feel better? Did you drink enough water?

What foods did you eat that caused you to feel worse?

How do you want tomorrow to be different?

What tiny (baby) steps would you like to take tomorrow for improved health, self-care, and that will move your life dreams and goals forward?

Circle or shade in how you feel today with one of the three face icons:

What are you most proud of about yourself for today?

Notes, brainstorming ideas or doodles:

Date   Day   Daily Intention
_____   _____   _____

How did you feel when you first woke up this morning?

How did you feel in your dreams last night?

What intuitive messages does your higher self (your soul) want you to know today?

What signs or symbols did you encounter or receive? What intuitive messages do you get through those signs or symbols you encountered?

Describe any people you encountered or circumstances that happened today that drained your energy:

How did you feel after this happened, what were your thoughts, and how was your body left feeling?

What spiritual cleansing, energetic cord cutting, energy healing, chakra clearing, visualization, mantra, prayer or meditation method did you use to clear the residual energy afterward from your body and auric field?

- [ ] Spiritual Cleansing
- [ ] Energy Healing
- [ ] Mantras
- [ ] Meditation
- [ ] Other
- [ ] Energetic Cord Cutting
- [ ] Chakra Clearing
- [ ] Visualization
- [ ] Prayers

What body sensations, intuitive thoughts or emotions did you feel today that helped you know you are going in the right direction for you?

What body sensations, intuitive thoughts or emotions did you feel today that helped you know you could be "off track" and need to take a step back?

What (pure) whole, nutritious foods did you eat that helped you feel better? Did you drink enough water?

What foods did you eat that caused you to feel worse?

How do you want tomorrow to be different?

What tiny (baby) steps would you like to take tomorrow for improved health, self-care, and that will move your life dreams and goals forward?

Circle or shade in how you feel today with one of the three face icons:

What are you most proud of about yourself for today?

Notes, brainstorming ideas or doodles:

Date _____ Day _____ Daily Intention _____

How did you feel when you first woke up this morning?

How did you feel in your dreams last night?

What intuitive messages does your higher self (your soul) want you to know today?

What signs or symbols did you encounter or receive? What intuitive messages do you get through those signs or symbols you encountered?

Describe any people you encountered or circumstances that happened today that drained your energy:

How did you feel after this happened, what were your thoughts, and how was your body left feeling?

What spiritual cleansing, energetic cord cutting, energy healing, chakra clearing, visualization, mantra, prayer or meditation method did you use to clear the residual energy afterward from your body and auric field?

- [ ] Spiritual Cleansing
- [ ] Energy Healing
- [ ] Mantras
- [ ] Meditation
- [ ] Other
- [ ] Energetic Cord Cutting
- [ ] Chakra Clearing
- [ ] Visualization
- [ ] Prayers

What body sensations, intuitive thoughts or emotions did you feel today that helped you know you are going in the right direction for you?

What body sensations, intuitive thoughts or emotions did you feel today that helped you know you could be "off track" and need to take a step back?

What (pure) whole, nutritious foods did you eat that helped you feel better? Did you drink enough water?

What foods did you eat that caused you to feel worse?

How do you want tomorrow to be different?

What tiny (baby) steps would you like to take tomorrow for improved health, self-care, and that will move your life dreams and goals forward?

Circle or shade in how you feel today with one of the three face icons:

What are you most proud of about yourself for today?

Notes, brainstorming ideas or doodles:

Date _____   Day _____   Daily Intention _____

How did you feel when you first woke up this morning?

How did you feel in your dreams last night?

What intuitive messages does your higher self (your soul) want you to know today?

What signs or symbols did you encounter or receive? What intuitive messages do you get through those signs or symbols you encountered?

Describe any people you encountered or circumstances that happened today that drained your energy:

How did you feel after this happened, what were your thoughts, and how was your body left feeling?

What spiritual cleansing, energetic cord cutting, energy healing, chakra clearing, visualization, mantra, prayer or meditation method did you use to clear the residual energy afterward from your body and auric field?

- [ ] Spiritual Cleansing
- [ ] Energy Healing
- [ ] Mantras
- [ ] Meditation
- [ ] Other
- [ ] Energetic Cord Cutting
- [ ] Chakra Clearing
- [ ] Visualization
- [ ] Prayers

What body sensations, intuitive thoughts or emotions did you feel today that helped you know you are going in the right direction for you?

What body sensations, intuitive thoughts or emotions did you feel today that helped you know you could be "off track" and need to take a step back?

What (pure) whole, nutritious foods did you eat that helped you feel better? Did you drink enough water?

What foods did you eat that caused you to feel worse?

How do you want tomorrow to be different?

What tiny (baby) steps would you like to take tomorrow for improved health, self-care, and that will move your life dreams and goals forward?

Circle or shade in how you feel today with one of the three face icons:

What are you most proud of about yourself for today?

Notes, brainstorming ideas or doodles:

Date _____ Day _____ Daily Intention _____

How did you feel when you first woke up this morning?

How did you feel in your dreams last night?

What intuitive messages does your higher self (your soul) want you to know today?

What signs or symbols did you encounter or receive? What intuitive messages do you get through those signs or symbols you encountered?

Describe any people you encountered or circumstances that happened today that drained your energy:

How did you feel after this happened, what were your thoughts, and how was your body left feeling?

What spiritual cleansing, energetic cord cutting, energy healing, chakra clearing, visualization, mantra, prayer or meditation method did you use to clear the residual energy afterward from your body and auric field?

- [ ] Spiritual Cleansing
- [ ] Energy Healing
- [ ] Mantras
- [ ] Meditation
- [ ] Other
- [ ] Energetic Cord Cutting
- [ ] Chakra Clearing
- [ ] Visualization
- [ ] Prayers

What body sensations, intuitive thoughts or emotions did you feel today that helped you know you are going in the right direction for you?

What body sensations, intuitive thoughts or emotions did you feel today that helped you know you could be "off track" and need to take a step back?

What (pure) whole, nutritious foods did you eat that helped you feel better? Did you drink enough water?

What foods did you eat that caused you to feel worse?

How do you want tomorrow to be different?

What tiny (baby) steps would you like to take tomorrow for improved health, self-care, and that will move your life dreams and goals forward?

Circle or shade in how you feel today with one of the three face icons:

What are you most proud of about yourself for today?

Notes, brainstorming ideas or doodles:

Date _____   Day _____   Daily Intention _____

How did you feel when you first woke up this morning?

How did you feel in your dreams last night?

What intuitive messages does your higher self (your soul) want you to know today?

What signs or symbols did you encounter or receive? What intuitive messages do you get through those signs or symbols you encountered?

Describe any people you encountered or circumstances that happened today that drained your energy:

How did you feel after this happened, what were your thoughts, and how was your body left feeling?

What spiritual cleansing, energetic cord cutting, energy healing, chakra clearing, visualization, mantra, prayer or meditation method did you use to clear the residual energy afterward from your body and auric field?

- [ ] Spiritual Cleansing
- [ ] Energy Healing
- [ ] Mantras
- [ ] Meditation
- [ ] Other
- [ ] Energetic Cord Cutting
- [ ] Chakra Clearing
- [ ] Visualization
- [ ] Prayers

What body sensations, intuitive thoughts or emotions did you feel today that helped you know you are going in the right direction for you?

What body sensations, intuitive thoughts or emotions did you feel today that helped you know you could be "off track" and need to take a step back?

What (pure) whole, nutritious foods did you eat that helped you feel better? Did you drink enough water?

What foods did you eat that caused you to feel worse?

How do you want tomorrow to be different?

What tiny (baby) steps would you like to take tomorrow for improved health, self-care, and that will move your life dreams and goals forward?

Circle or shade in how you feel today with one of the three face icons:

What are you most proud of about yourself for today?

Notes, brainstorming ideas or doodles:

Date   Day   Daily Intention
_____   _____   _____

How did you feel when you first woke up this morning?

How did you feel in your dreams last night?

What intuitive messages does your higher self (your soul) want you to know today?

What signs or symbols did you encounter or receive? What intuitive messages do you get through those signs or symbols you encountered?

Describe any people you encountered or circumstances that happened today that drained your energy:

How did you feel after this happened, what were your thoughts, and how was your body left feeling?

What spiritual cleansing, energetic cord cutting, energy healing, chakra clearing, visualization, mantra, prayer or meditation method did you use to clear the residual energy afterward from your body and auric field?

- [ ] Spiritual Cleansing
- [ ] Energy Healing
- [ ] Mantras
- [ ] Meditation
- [ ] Other
- [ ] Energetic Cord Cutting
- [ ] Chakra Clearing
- [ ] Visualization
- [ ] Prayers

What body sensations, intuitive thoughts or emotions did you feel today that helped you know you are going in the right direction for you?

What body sensations, intuitive thoughts or emotions did you feel today that helped you know you could be "off track" and need to take a step back?

What (pure) whole, nutritious foods did you eat that helped you feel better? Did you drink enough water?

what foods did you eat that caused you to feel worse?

How do you want tomorrow to be different?

what tiny (baby) steps would you like to take tomorrow for improved health, self-care, and that will move your life dreams and goals forward?

Circle or shade in how you feel today with one of the three face icons:

what are you most proud of about yourself for today?

Notes, brainstorming ideas or doodles:

Date _____   Day _____   Daily Intention _____

How did you feel when you first woke up this morning?

How did you feel in your dreams last night?

What intuitive messages does your higher self (your soul) want you to know today?

What signs or symbols did you encounter or receive? What intuitive messages do you get through those signs or symbols you encountered?

Describe any people you encountered or circumstances that happened today that drained your energy:

How did you feel after this happened, what were your thoughts, and how was your body left feeling?

What spiritual cleansing, energetic cord cutting, energy healing, chakra clearing, visualization, mantra, prayer or meditation method did you use to clear the residual energy afterward from your body and auric field?

- [ ] Spiritual Cleansing
- [ ] Energy Healing
- [ ] Mantras
- [ ] Meditation
- [ ] Other
- [ ] Energetic Cord Cutting
- [ ] Chakra Clearing
- [ ] Visualization
- [ ] Prayers

What body sensations, intuitive thoughts or emotions did you feel today that helped you know you are going in the right direction for you?

What body sensations, intuitive thoughts or emotions did you feel today that helped you know you could be "off track" and need to take a step back?

What (pure) whole, nutritious foods did you eat that helped you feel better? Did you drink enough water?

What foods did you eat that caused you to feel worse?

How do you want tomorrow to be different?

What tiny (baby) steps would you like to take tomorrow for improved health, self-care, and that will move your life dreams and goals forward?

Circle or shade in how you feel today with one of the three face icons:

What are you most proud of about yourself for today?

Notes, brainstorming ideas or doodles:

Date _____   Day _____   Daily Intention _____

How did you feel when you first woke up this morning?

How did you feel in your dreams last night?

What intuitive messages does your higher self (your soul) want you to know today?

What signs or symbols did you encounter or receive? What intuitive messages do you get through those signs or symbols you encountered?

Describe any people you encountered or circumstances that happened today that drained your energy:

How did you feel after this happened, what were your thoughts, and how was your body left feeling?

What spiritual cleansing, energetic cord cutting, energy healing, chakra clearing, visualization, mantra, prayer or meditation method did you use to clear the residual energy afterward from your body and auric field?

- [ ] Spiritual Cleansing
- [ ] Energy Healing
- [ ] Mantras
- [ ] Meditation
- [ ] Other
- [ ] Energetic Cord Cutting
- [ ] Chakra Clearing
- [ ] Visualization
- [ ] Prayers

What body sensations, intuitive thoughts or emotions did you feel today that helped you know you are going in the right direction for you?

What body sensations, intuitive thoughts or emotions did you feel today that helped you know you could be "off track" and need to take a step back?

What (pure) whole, nutritious foods did you eat that helped you feel better? Did you drink enough water?

What foods did you eat that caused you to feel worse?

How do you want tomorrow to be different?

What tiny (baby) steps would you like to take tomorrow for improved health, self-care, and that will move your life dreams and goals forward?

Circle or shade in how you feel today with one of the three face icons:

What are you most proud of about yourself for today?

Notes, brainstorming ideas or doodles:

Date _____   Day _____   Daily Intention _____

How did you feel when you first woke up this morning?

How did you feel in your dreams last night?

What intuitive messages does your higher self (your soul) want you to know today?

What signs or symbols did you encounter or receive? What intuitive messages do you get through those signs or symbols you encountered?

Describe any people you encountered or circumstances that happened today that drained your energy:

How did you feel after this happened, what were your thoughts, and how was your body left feeling?

What spiritual cleansing, energetic cord cutting, energy healing, chakra clearing, visualization, mantra, prayer or meditation method did you use to clear the residual energy afterward from your body and auric field?

- [ ] Spiritual Cleansing
- [ ] Energy Healing
- [ ] Mantras
- [ ] Meditation
- [ ] Other
- [ ] Energetic Cord Cutting
- [ ] Chakra Clearing
- [ ] Visualization
- [ ] Prayers

What body sensations, intuitive thoughts or emotions did you feel today that helped you know you are going in the right direction for you?

What body sensations, intuitive thoughts or emotions did you feel today that helped you know you could be "off track" and need to take a step back?

What (pure) whole, nutritious foods did you eat that helped you feel better? Did you drink enough water?

what foods did you eat that caused you to feel worse?

How do you want tomorrow to be different?

what tiny (baby) steps would you like to take tomorrow for improved health, self-care, and that will move your life dreams and goals forward?

Circle or shade in how you feel today with one of the three face icons:

What are you most proud of about yourself for today?

Notes, brainstorming ideas or doodles:

Date _____   Day _____   Daily Intention _____

How did you feel when you first woke up this morning?

How did you feel in your dreams last night?

What intuitive messages does your higher self (your soul) want you to know today?

What signs or symbols did you encounter or receive? What intuitive messages do you get through those signs or symbols you encountered?

Describe any people you encountered or circumstances that happened today that drained your energy:

How did you feel after this happened, what were your thoughts, and how was your body left feeling?

What spiritual cleansing, energetic cord cutting, energy healing, chakra clearing, visualization, mantra, prayer or meditation method did you use to clear the residual energy afterward from your body and auric field?

- [ ] Spiritual Cleansing
- [ ] Energy Healing
- [ ] Mantras
- [ ] Meditation
- [ ] Other
- [ ] Energetic Cord Cutting
- [ ] Chakra Clearing
- [ ] Visualization
- [ ] Prayers

What body sensations, intuitive thoughts or emotions did you feel today that helped you know you are going in the right direction for you?

What body sensations, intuitive thoughts or emotions did you feel today that helped you know you could be "off track" and need to take a step back?

What (pure) whole, nutritious foods did you eat that helped you feel better? Did you drink enough water?

What foods did you eat that caused you to feel worse?

How do you want tomorrow to be different?

What tiny (baby) steps would you like to take tomorrow for improved health, self-care, and that will move your life dreams and goals forward?

Circle or shade in how you feel today with one of the three face icons:

What are you most proud of about yourself for today?

Notes, brainstorming ideas or doodles:

Date   Day   Daily Intention

How did you feel when you first woke up this morning?

How did you feel in your dreams last night?

What intuitive messages does your higher self (your soul) want you to know today?

What signs or symbols did you encounter or receive? What intuitive messages do you get through those signs or symbols you encountered?

Describe any people you encountered or circumstances that happened today that drained your energy:

How did you feel after this happened, what were your thoughts, and how was your body left feeling?

What spiritual cleansing, energetic cord cutting, energy healing, chakra clearing, visualization, mantra, prayer or meditation method did you use to clear the residual energy afterward from your body and auric field?

- [ ] Spiritual Cleansing
- [ ] Energy Healing
- [ ] Mantras
- [ ] Meditation
- [ ] Other
- [ ] Energetic Cord Cutting
- [ ] Chakra Clearing
- [ ] Visualization
- [ ] Prayers

What body sensations, intuitive thoughts or emotions did you feel today that helped you know you are going in the right direction for you?

What body sensations, intuitive thoughts or emotions did you feel today that helped you know you could be "off track" and need to take a step back?

What (pure) whole, nutritious foods did you eat that helped you feel better? Did you drink enough water?

What foods did you eat that caused you to feel worse?

How do you want tomorrow to be different?

What tiny (baby) steps would you like to take tomorrow for improved health, self-care, and that will move your life dreams and goals forward?

Circle or shade in how you feel today with one of the three face icons:

What are you most proud of about yourself for today?

Notes, brainstorming ideas or doodles:

Date _____   Day _____   Daily Intention _____

How did you feel when you first woke up this morning?

How did you feel in your dreams last night?

What intuitive messages does your higher self (your soul) want you to know today?

What signs or symbols did you encounter or receive? What intuitive messages do you get through those signs or symbols you encountered?

Describe any people you encountered or circumstances that happened today that drained your energy:

How did you feel after this happened, what were your thoughts, and how was your body left feeling?

What spiritual cleansing, energetic cord cutting, energy healing, chakra clearing, visualization, mantra, prayer or meditation method did you use to clear the residual energy afterward from your body and auric field?

- [ ] Spiritual Cleansing
- [ ] Energy Healing
- [ ] Mantras
- [ ] Meditation
- [ ] Other
- [ ] Energetic Cord Cutting
- [ ] Chakra Clearing
- [ ] Visualization
- [ ] Prayers

What body sensations, intuitive thoughts or emotions did you feel today that helped you know you are going in the right direction for you?

What body sensations, intuitive thoughts or emotions did you feel today that helped you know you could be "off track" and need to take a step back?

What (pure) whole, nutritious foods did you eat that helped you feel better? Did you drink enough water?

What foods did you eat that caused you to feel worse?

How do you want tomorrow to be different?

What tiny (baby) steps would you like to take tomorrow for improved health, self-care, and that will move your life dreams and goals forward?

Circle or shade in how you feel today with one of the three face icons:

What are you most proud of about yourself for today?

Notes, brainstorming ideas or doodles:

Date   Day   Daily Intention
_____   _____   _____

How did you feel when you first woke up this morning?

How did you feel in your dreams last night?

What intuitive messages does your higher self (your soul) want you to know today?

What signs or symbols did you encounter or receive? What intuitive messages do you get through those signs or symbols you encountered?

Describe any people you encountered or circumstances that happened today that drained your energy:

How did you feel after this happened, what were your thoughts, and how was your body left feeling?

What spiritual cleansing, energetic cord cutting, energy healing, chakra clearing, visualization, mantra, prayer or meditation method did you use to clear the residual energy afterward from your body and auric field?

- [ ] Spiritual Cleansing
- [ ] Energy Healing
- [ ] Mantras
- [ ] Meditation
- [ ] Other
- [ ] Energetic Cord Cutting
- [ ] Chakra Clearing
- [ ] Visualization
- [ ] Prayers

What body sensations, intuitive thoughts or emotions did you feel today that helped you know you are going in the right direction for you?

What body sensations, intuitive thoughts or emotions did you feel today that helped you know you could be "off track" and need to take a step back?

What (pure) whole, nutritious foods did you eat that helped you feel better? Did you drink enough water?

What foods did you eat that caused you to feel worse?

How do you want tomorrow to be different?

What tiny (baby) steps would you like to take tomorrow for improved health, self-care, and that will move your life dreams and goals forward?

Circle or shade in how you feel today with one of the three face icons:

What are you most proud of about yourself for today?

Notes, brainstorming ideas or doodles:

Date   Day   Daily Intention
_____   _____   _____

How did you feel when you first woke up this morning?

How did you feel in your dreams last night?

What intuitive messages does your higher self (your soul) want you to know today?

What signs or symbols did you encounter or receive? What intuitive messages do you get through those signs or symbols you encountered?

Describe any people you encountered or circumstances that happened today that drained your energy:

How did you feel after this happened, what were your thoughts, and how was your body left feeling?

What spiritual cleansing, energetic cord cutting, energy healing, chakra clearing, visualization, mantra, prayer or meditation method did you use to clear the residual energy afterward from your body and auric field?

- [ ] Spiritual Cleansing
- [ ] Energy Healing
- [ ] Mantras
- [ ] Meditation
- [ ] Other
- [ ] Energetic Cord Cutting
- [ ] Chakra Clearing
- [ ] Visualization
- [ ] Prayers

What body sensations, intuitive thoughts or emotions did you feel today that helped you know you are going in the right direction for you?

What body sensations, intuitive thoughts or emotions did you feel today that helped you know you could be "off track" and need to take a step back?

What (pure) whole, nutritious foods did you eat that helped you feel better? Did you drink enough water?

what foods did you eat that caused you to feel worse?

How do you want tomorrow to be different?

What tiny (baby) steps would you like to take tomorrow for improved health, self-care, and that will move your life dreams and goals forward?

Circle or shade in how you feel today with one of the three face icons:

What are you most proud of about yourself for today?

Notes, brainstorming ideas or doodles:

Date	Day	Daily Intention

How did you feel when you first woke up this morning?

How did you feel in your dreams last night?

What intuitive messages does your higher self (your soul) want you to know today?

What signs or symbols did you encounter or receive? What intuitive messages do you get through those signs or symbols you encountered?

Describe any people you encountered or circumstances that happened today that drained your energy:

How did you feel after this happened, what were your thoughts, and how was your body left feeling?

What spiritual cleansing, energetic cord cutting, energy healing, chakra clearing, visualization, mantra, prayer or meditation method did you use to clear the residual energy afterward from your body and auric field?

- [ ] Spiritual Cleansing
- [ ] Energy Healing
- [ ] Mantras
- [ ] Meditation
- [ ] Other
- [ ] Energetic Cord Cutting
- [ ] Chakra Clearing
- [ ] Visualization
- [ ] Prayers

What body sensations, intuitive thoughts or emotions did you feel today that helped you know you are going in the right direction for you?

What body sensations, intuitive thoughts or emotions did you feel today that helped you know you could be "off track" and need to take a step back?

What (pure) whole, nutritious foods did you eat that helped you feel better? Did you drink enough water?

What foods did you eat that caused you to feel worse?

How do you want tomorrow to be different?

What tiny (baby) steps would you like to take tomorrow for improved health, self-care, and that will move your life dreams and goals forward?

Circle or shade in how you feel today with one of the three face icons:

What are you most proud of about yourself for today?

Notes, brainstorming ideas or doodles:

Date _____ Day _____ Daily Intention _____

How did you feel when you first woke up this morning?

How did you feel in your dreams last night?

What intuitive messages does your higher self (your soul) want you to know today?

What signs or symbols did you encounter or receive? What intuitive messages do you get through those signs or symbols you encountered?

Describe any people you encountered or circumstances that happened today that drained your energy:

How did you feel after this happened, what were your thoughts, and how was your body left feeling?

What spiritual cleansing, energetic cord cutting, energy healing, chakra clearing, visualization, mantra, prayer or meditation method did you use to clear the residual energy afterward from your body and auric field?

- [ ] Spiritual Cleansing
- [ ] Energy Healing
- [ ] Mantras
- [ ] Meditation
- [ ] Other
- [ ] Energetic Cord Cutting
- [ ] Chakra Clearing
- [ ] Visualization
- [ ] Prayers

What body sensations, intuitive thoughts or emotions did you feel today that helped you know you are going in the right direction for you?

What body sensations, intuitive thoughts or emotions did you feel today that helped you know you could be "off track" and need to take a step back?

What (pure) whole, nutritious foods did you eat that helped you feel better? Did you drink enough water?

What foods did you eat that caused you to feel worse?

How do you want tomorrow to be different?

What tiny (baby) steps would you like to take tomorrow for improved health, self-care, and that will move your life dreams and goals forward?

Circle or shade in how you feel today with one of the three face icons:

What are you most proud of about yourself for today?

Notes, brainstorming ideas or doodles:

Date _____   Day _____   Daily Intention _____

How did you feel when you first woke up this morning?

How did you feel in your dreams last night?

What intuitive messages does your higher self (your soul) want you to know today?

What signs or symbols did you encounter or receive? What intuitive messages do you get through those signs or symbols you encountered?

Describe any people you encountered or circumstances that happened today that drained your energy:

How did you feel after this happened, what were your thoughts, and how was your body left feeling?

What spiritual cleansing, energetic cord cutting, energy healing, chakra clearing, visualization, mantra, prayer or meditation method did you use to clear the residual energy afterward from your body and auric field?

- [ ] Spiritual Cleansing
- [ ] Energy Healing
- [ ] Mantras
- [ ] Meditation
- [ ] Other
- [ ] Energetic Cord Cutting
- [ ] Chakra Clearing
- [ ] Visualization
- [ ] Prayers

What body sensations, intuitive thoughts or emotions did you feel today that helped you know you are going in the right direction for you?

What body sensations, intuitive thoughts or emotions did you feel today that helped you know you could be "off track" and need to take a step back?

What (pure) whole, nutritious foods did you eat that helped you feel better? Did you drink enough water?

what foods did you eat that caused you to feel worse?

How do you want tomorrow to be different?

what tiny (baby) steps would you like to take tomorrow for improved health, self-care, and that will move your life dreams and goals forward?

Circle or shade in how you feel today with one of the three face icons:

What are you most proud of about yourself for today?

Notes, brainstorming ideas or doodles:

Date _____   Day _____   Daily Intention _____

How did you feel when you first woke up this morning?

How did you feel in your dreams last night?

What intuitive messages does your higher self (your soul) want you to know today?

What signs or symbols did you encounter or receive? What intuitive messages do you get through those signs or symbols you encountered?

Describe any people you encountered or circumstances that happened today that drained your energy:

How did you feel after this happened, what were your thoughts, and how was your body left feeling?

What spiritual cleansing, energetic cord cutting, energy healing, chakra clearing, visualization, mantra, prayer or meditation method did you use to clear the residual energy afterward from your body and auric field?

- [ ] Spiritual Cleansing
- [ ] Energy Healing
- [ ] Mantras
- [ ] Meditation
- [ ] Other
- [ ] Energetic Cord Cutting
- [ ] Chakra Clearing
- [ ] Visualization
- [ ] Prayers

What body sensations, intuitive thoughts or emotions did you feel today that helped you know you are going in the right direction for you?

What body sensations, intuitive thoughts or emotions did you feel today that helped you know you could be "off track" and need to take a step back?

What (pure) whole, nutritious foods did you eat that helped you feel better? Did you drink enough water?

What foods did you eat that caused you to feel worse?

How do you want tomorrow to be different?

What tiny (baby) steps would you like to take tomorrow for improved health, self-care, and that will move your life dreams and goals forward?

Circle or shade in how you feel today with one of the three face icons:

What are you most proud of about yourself for today?

Notes, brainstorming ideas or doodles:

Date _____ Day _____ Daily Intention _____

How did you feel when you first woke up this morning?

How did you feel in your dreams last night?

What intuitive messages does your higher self (your soul) want you to know today?

What signs or symbols did you encounter or receive? What intuitive messages do you get through those signs or symbols you encountered?

Describe any people you encountered or circumstances that happened today that drained your energy:

How did you feel after this happened, what were your thoughts, and how was your body left feeling?

What spiritual cleansing, energetic cord cutting, energy healing, chakra clearing, visualization, mantra, prayer or meditation method did you use to clear the residual energy afterward from your body and auric field?

- [ ] Spiritual Cleansing
- [ ] Energy Healing
- [ ] Mantras
- [ ] Meditation
- [ ] Other
- [ ] Energetic Cord Cutting
- [ ] Chakra Clearing
- [ ] Visualization
- [ ] Prayers

What body sensations, intuitive thoughts or emotions did you feel today that helped you know you are going in the right direction for you?

What body sensations, intuitive thoughts or emotions did you feel today that helped you know you could be "off track" and need to take a step back?

What (pure) whole, nutritious foods did you eat that helped you feel better? Did you drink enough water?

what foods did you eat that caused you to feel worse?

How do you want tomorrow to be different?

what tiny (baby) steps would you like to take tomorrow for improved health, self-care, and that will move your life dreams and goals forward?

Circle or shade in how you feel today with one of the three face icons:

what are you most proud of about yourself for today?

Notes, brainstorming ideas or doodles:

Date　　　　Day　　　　Daily Intention
_____　_____　_____

How did you feel when you first woke up this morning?

How did you feel in your dreams last night?

What intuitive messages does your higher self (your soul) want you to know today?

What signs or symbols did you encounter or receive? What intuitive messages do you get through those signs or symbols you encountered?

Describe any people you encountered or circumstances that happened today that drained your energy:

How did you feel after this happened, what were your thoughts, and how was your body left feeling?

What spiritual cleansing, energetic cord cutting, energy healing, chakra clearing, visualization, mantra, prayer or meditation method did you use to clear the residual energy afterward from your body and auric field?

- [ ] Spiritual Cleansing
- [ ] Energy Healing
- [ ] Mantras
- [ ] Meditation
- [ ] Other
- [ ] Energetic Cord Cutting
- [ ] Chakra Clearing
- [ ] Visualization
- [ ] Prayers

What body sensations, intuitive thoughts or emotions did you feel today that helped you know you are going in the right direction for you?

What body sensations, intuitive thoughts or emotions did you feel today that helped you know you could be "off track" and need to take a step back?

What (pure) whole, nutritious foods did you eat that helped you feel better? Did you drink enough water?

what foods did you eat that caused you to feel worse?

How do you want tomorrow to be different?

what tiny (baby) steps would you like to take tomorrow for improved health, self-care, and that will move your life dreams and goals forward?

Circle or shade in how you feel today with one of the three face icons:

What are you most proud of about yourself for today?

Notes, brainstorming ideas or doodles:

Date   Day   Daily Intention

How did you feel when you first woke up this morning?

How did you feel in your dreams last night?

What intuitive messages does your higher self (your soul) want you to know today?

What signs or symbols did you encounter or receive? What intuitive messages do you get through those signs or symbols you encountered?

Describe any people you encountered or circumstances that happened today that drained your energy:

How did you feel after this happened, what were your thoughts, and how was your body left feeling?

What spiritual cleansing, energetic cord cutting, energy healing, chakra clearing, visualization, mantra, prayer or meditation method did you use to clear the residual energy afterward from your body and auric field?

- [ ] Spiritual Cleansing
- [ ] Energy Healing
- [ ] Mantras
- [ ] Meditation
- [ ] Other
- [ ] Energetic Cord Cutting
- [ ] Chakra Clearing
- [ ] Visualization
- [ ] Prayers

What body sensations, intuitive thoughts or emotions did you feel today that helped you know you are going in the right direction for you?

What body sensations, intuitive thoughts or emotions did you feel today that helped you know you could be "off track" and need to take a step back?

What (pure) whole, nutritious foods did you eat that helped you feel better? Did you drink enough water?

what foods did you eat that caused you to feel worse?

How do you want tomorrow to be different?

What tiny (baby) steps would you like to take tomorrow for improved health, self-care, and that will move your life dreams and goals forward?

Circle or shade in how you feel today with one of the three face icons:

what are you most proud of about yourself for today?

Notes, brainstorming ideas or doodles:

Date _____   Day _____   Daily Intention _____

How did you feel when you first woke up this morning?

How did you feel in your dreams last night?

What intuitive messages does your higher self (your soul) want you to know today?

What signs or symbols did you encounter or receive? What intuitive messages do you get through those signs or symbols you encountered?

Describe any people you encountered or circumstances that happened today that drained your energy:

How did you feel after this happened, what were your thoughts, and how was your body left feeling?

What spiritual cleansing, energetic cord cutting, energy healing, chakra clearing, visualization, mantra, prayer or meditation method did you use to clear the residual energy afterward from your body and auric field?

- [ ] Spiritual Cleansing
- [ ] Energy Healing
- [ ] Mantras
- [ ] Meditation
- [ ] Other
- [ ] Energetic Cord Cutting
- [ ] Chakra Clearing
- [ ] Visualization
- [ ] Prayers

What body sensations, intuitive thoughts or emotions did you feel today that helped you know you are going in the right direction for you?

What body sensations, intuitive thoughts or emotions did you feel today that helped you know you could be "off track" and need to take a step back?

What (pure) whole, nutritious foods did you eat that helped you feel better? Did you drink enough water?

What foods did you eat that caused you to feel worse?

How do you want tomorrow to be different?

What tiny (baby) steps would you like to take tomorrow for improved health, self-care, and that will move your life dreams and goals forward?

Circle or shade in how you feel today with one of the three face icons:

What are you most proud of about yourself for today?

Notes, brainstorming ideas or doodles:

Date _____ Day _____ Daily Intention _____

How did you feel when you first woke up this morning?

How did you feel in your dreams last night?

What intuitive messages does your higher self (your soul) want you to know today?

What signs or symbols did you encounter or receive? What intuitive messages do you get through those signs or symbols you encountered?

Describe any people you encountered or circumstances that happened today that drained your energy:

How did you feel after this happened, what were your thoughts, and how was your body left feeling?

What spiritual cleansing, energetic cord cutting, energy healing, chakra clearing, visualization, mantra, prayer or meditation method did you use to clear the residual energy afterward from your body and auric field?

- [ ] Spiritual Cleansing
- [ ] Energy Healing
- [ ] Mantras
- [ ] Meditation
- [ ] Other
- [ ] Energetic Cord Cutting
- [ ] Chakra Clearing
- [ ] Visualization
- [ ] Prayers

What body sensations, intuitive thoughts or emotions did you feel today that helped you know you are going in the right direction for you?

What body sensations, intuitive thoughts or emotions did you feel today that helped you know you could be "off track" and need to take a step back?

What (pure) whole, nutritious foods did you eat that helped you feel better? Did you drink enough water?

What foods did you eat that caused you to feel worse?

How do you want tomorrow to be different?

What tiny (baby) steps would you like to take tomorrow for improved health, self-care, and that will move your life dreams and goals forward?

Circle or shade in how you feel today with one of the three face icons:

What are you most proud of about yourself for today?

Notes, brainstorming ideas or doodles:

Date   Day   Daily Intention

How did you feel when you first woke up this morning?

How did you feel in your dreams last night?

What intuitive messages does your higher self (your soul) want you to know today?

What signs or symbols did you encounter or receive? What intuitive messages do you get through those signs or symbols you encountered?

Describe any people you encountered or circumstances that happened today that drained your energy:

How did you feel after this happened, what were your thoughts, and how was your body left feeling?

What spiritual cleansing, energetic cord cutting, energy healing, chakra clearing, visualization, mantra, prayer or meditation method did you use to clear the residual energy afterward from your body and auric field?

- [ ] Spiritual Cleansing
- [ ] Energy Healing
- [ ] Mantras
- [ ] Meditation
- [ ] Other
- [ ] Energetic Cord Cutting
- [ ] Chakra Clearing
- [ ] Visualization
- [ ] Prayers

What body sensations, intuitive thoughts or emotions did you feel today that helped you know you are going in the right direction for you?

What body sensations, intuitive thoughts or emotions did you feel today that helped you know you could be "off track" and need to take a step back?

What (pure) whole, nutritious foods did you eat that helped you feel better? Did you drink enough water?

what foods did you eat that caused you to feel worse?

How do you want tomorrow to be different?

what tiny (baby) steps would you like to take tomorrow for improved health, self-care, and that will move your life dreams and goals forward?

Circle or shade in how you feel today with one of the three face icons:

what are you most proud of about yourself for today?

Notes, brainstorming ideas or doodles:

Date _____   Day _____   Daily Intention _____

How did you feel when you first woke up this morning?

How did you feel in your dreams last night?

What intuitive messages does your higher self (your soul) want you to know today?

What signs or symbols did you encounter or receive? What intuitive messages do you get through those signs or symbols you encountered?

Describe any people you encountered or circumstances that happened today that drained your energy:

How did you feel after this happened, what were your thoughts, and how was your body left feeling?

What spiritual cleansing, energetic cord cutting, energy healing, chakra clearing, visualization, mantra, prayer or meditation method did you use to clear the residual energy afterward from your body and auric field?

- [ ] Spiritual Cleansing
- [ ] Energy Healing
- [ ] Mantras
- [ ] Meditation
- [ ] Other
- [ ] Energetic Cord Cutting
- [ ] Chakra Clearing
- [ ] Visualization
- [ ] Prayers

What body sensations, intuitive thoughts or emotions did you feel today that helped you know you are going in the right direction for you?

What body sensations, intuitive thoughts or emotions did you feel today that helped you know you could be "off track" and need to take a step back?

What (pure) whole, nutritious foods did you eat that helped you feel better? Did you drink enough water?

What foods did you eat that caused you to feel worse?

How do you want tomorrow to be different?

What tiny (baby) steps would you like to take tomorrow for improved health, self-care, and that will move your life dreams and goals forward?

Circle or shade in how you feel today with one of the three face icons:

What are you most proud of about yourself for today?

Notes, brainstorming ideas or doodles:

Date   Day   Daily Intention

How did you feel when you first woke up this morning?

How did you feel in your dreams last night?

What intuitive messages does your higher self (your soul) want you to know today?

What signs or symbols did you encounter or receive? What intuitive messages do you get through those signs or symbols you encountered?

Describe any people you encountered or circumstances that happened today that drained your energy:

How did you feel after this happened, what were your thoughts, and how was your body left feeling?

What spiritual cleansing, energetic cord cutting, energy healing, chakra clearing, visualization, mantra, prayer or meditation method did you use to clear the residual energy afterward from your body and auric field?

- [ ] Spiritual Cleansing
- [ ] Energy Healing
- [ ] Mantras
- [ ] Meditation
- [ ] Other
- [ ] Energetic Cord Cutting
- [ ] Chakra Clearing
- [ ] Visualization
- [ ] Prayers

What body sensations, intuitive thoughts or emotions did you feel today that helped you know you are going in the right direction for you?

What body sensations, intuitive thoughts or emotions did you feel today that helped you know you could be "off track" and need to take a step back?

What (pure) whole, nutritious foods did you eat that helped you feel better? Did you drink enough water?

What foods did you eat that caused you to feel worse?

How do you want tomorrow to be different?

What tiny (baby) steps would you like to take tomorrow for improved health, self-care, and that will move your life dreams and goals forward?

Circle or shade in how you feel today with one of the three face icons:

What are you most proud of about yourself for today?

Notes, brainstorming ideas or doodles:

Date _____ Day _____ Daily Intention _____

How did you feel when you first woke up this morning?

How did you feel in your dreams last night?

What intuitive messages does your higher self (your soul) want you to know today?

What signs or symbols did you encounter or receive? What intuitive messages do you get through those signs or symbols you encountered?

Describe any people you encountered or circumstances that happened today that drained your energy:

How did you feel after this happened, what were your thoughts, and how was your body left feeling?

What spiritual cleansing, energetic cord cutting, energy healing, chakra clearing, visualization, mantra, prayer or meditation method did you use to clear the residual energy afterward from your body and auric field?

- [ ] Spiritual Cleansing
- [ ] Energy Healing
- [ ] Mantras
- [ ] Meditation
- [ ] Other
- [ ] Energetic Cord Cutting
- [ ] Chakra Clearing
- [ ] Visualization
- [ ] Prayers

What body sensations, intuitive thoughts or emotions did you feel today that helped you know you are going in the right direction for you?

What body sensations, intuitive thoughts or emotions did you feel today that helped you know you could be "off track" and need to take a step back?

What (pure) whole, nutritious foods did you eat that helped you feel better? Did you drink enough water?

What foods did you eat that caused you to feel worse?

How do you want tomorrow to be different?

What tiny (baby) steps would you like to take tomorrow for improved health, self-care, and that will move your life dreams and goals forward?

Circle or shade in how you feel today with one of the three face icons:

What are you most proud of about yourself for today?

Notes, brainstorming ideas or doodles:

Date _____   Day _____   Daily Intention _____

How did you feel when you first woke up this morning?

How did you feel in your dreams last night?

What intuitive messages does your higher self (your soul) want you to know today?

What signs or symbols did you encounter or receive? What intuitive messages do you get through those signs or symbols you encountered?

Describe any people you encountered or circumstances that happened today that drained your energy:

How did you feel after this happened, what were your thoughts, and how was your body left feeling?

What spiritual cleansing, energetic cord cutting, energy healing, chakra clearing, visualization, mantra, prayer or meditation method did you use to clear the residual energy afterward from your body and auric field?

- [ ] Spiritual Cleansing
- [ ] Energy Healing
- [ ] Mantras
- [ ] Meditation
- [ ] Other
- [ ] Energetic Cord Cutting
- [ ] Chakra Clearing
- [ ] Visualization
- [ ] Prayers

What body sensations, intuitive thoughts or emotions did you feel today that helped you know you are going in the right direction for you?

What body sensations, intuitive thoughts or emotions did you feel today that helped you know you could be "off track" and need to take a step back?

What (pure) whole, nutritious foods did you eat that helped you feel better? Did you drink enough water?

What foods did you eat that caused you to feel worse?

How do you want tomorrow to be different?

What tiny (baby) steps would you like to take tomorrow for improved health, self-care, and that will move your life dreams and goals forward?

Circle or shade in how you feel today with one of the three face icons:

What are you most proud of about yourself for today?

Notes, brainstorming ideas or doodles:

Date   Day   Daily Intention

How did you feel when you first woke up this morning?

How did you feel in your dreams last night?

What intuitive messages does your higher self (your soul) want you to know today?

What signs or symbols did you encounter or receive? What intuitive messages do you get through those signs or symbols you encountered?

Describe any people you encountered or circumstances that happened today that drained your energy:

How did you feel after this happened, what were your thoughts, and how was your body left feeling?

What spiritual cleansing, energetic cord cutting, energy healing, chakra clearing, visualization, mantra, prayer or meditation method did you use to clear the residual energy afterward from your body and auric field?

- [ ] Spiritual Cleansing
- [ ] Energy Healing
- [ ] Mantras
- [ ] Meditation
- [ ] Other
- [ ] Energetic Cord Cutting
- [ ] Chakra Clearing
- [ ] Visualization
- [ ] Prayers

What body sensations, intuitive thoughts or emotions did you feel today that helped you know you are going in the right direction for you?

What body sensations, intuitive thoughts or emotions did you feel today that helped you know you could be "off track" and need to take a step back?

What (pure) whole, nutritious foods did you eat that helped you feel better? Did you drink enough water?

What foods did you eat that caused you to feel worse?

How do you want tomorrow to be different?

What tiny (baby) steps would you like to take tomorrow for improved health, self-care, and that will move your life dreams and goals forward?

Circle or shade in how you feel today with one of the three face icons:

What are you most proud of about yourself for today?

Notes, brainstorming ideas or doodles:

Date _____   Day _____   Daily Intention _____

How did you feel when you first woke up this morning?

How did you feel in your dreams last night?

What intuitive messages does your higher self (your soul) want you to know today?

What signs or symbols did you encounter or receive? What intuitive messages do you get through those signs or symbols you encountered?

Describe any people you encountered or circumstances that happened today that drained your energy:

How did you feel after this happened, what were your thoughts, and how was your body left feeling?

What spiritual cleansing, energetic cord cutting, energy healing, chakra clearing, visualization, mantra, prayer or meditation method did you use to clear the residual energy afterward from your body and auric field?

- [ ] Spiritual Cleansing
- [ ] Energy Healing
- [ ] Mantras
- [ ] Meditation
- [ ] Other
- [ ] Energetic Cord Cutting
- [ ] Chakra Clearing
- [ ] Visualization
- [ ] Prayers

What body sensations, intuitive thoughts or emotions did you feel today that helped you know you are going in the right direction for you?

What body sensations, intuitive thoughts or emotions did you feel today that helped you know you could be "off track" and need to take a step back?

What (pure) whole, nutritious foods did you eat that helped you feel better? Did you drink enough water?

What foods did you eat that caused you to feel worse?

How do you want tomorrow to be different?

What tiny (baby) steps would you like to take tomorrow for improved health, self-care, and that will move your life dreams and goals forward?

Circle or shade in how you feel today with one of the three face icons:

What are you most proud of about yourself for today?

Notes, brainstorming ideas or doodles:

Date _____   Day _____   Daily Intention _____

How did you feel when you first woke up this morning?

How did you feel in your dreams last night?

What intuitive messages does your higher self (your soul) want you to know today?

What signs or symbols did you encounter or receive? What intuitive messages do you get through those signs or symbols you encountered?

Describe any people you encountered or circumstances that happened today that drained your energy:

How did you feel after this happened, what were your thoughts, and how was your body left feeling?

What spiritual cleansing, energetic cord cutting, energy healing, chakra clearing, visualization, mantra, prayer or meditation method did you use to clear the residual energy afterward from your body and auric field?

- [ ] Spiritual Cleansing
- [ ] Energy Healing
- [ ] Mantras
- [ ] Meditation
- [ ] Other
- [ ] Energetic Cord Cutting
- [ ] Chakra Clearing
- [ ] Visualization
- [ ] Prayers

What body sensations, intuitive thoughts or emotions did you feel today that helped you know you are going in the right direction for you?

What body sensations, intuitive thoughts or emotions did you feel today that helped you know you could be "off track" and need to take a step back?

What (pure) whole, nutritious foods did you eat that helped you feel better? Did you drink enough water?

What foods did you eat that caused you to feel worse?

How do you want tomorrow to be different?

What tiny (baby) steps would you like to take tomorrow for improved health, self-care, and that will move your life dreams and goals forward?

Circle or shade in how you feel today with one of the three face icons:

What are you most proud of about yourself for today?

Notes, brainstorming ideas or doodles:

Date _____ Day _____ Daily Intention _____

How did you feel when you first woke up this morning?

How did you feel in your dreams last night?

What intuitive messages does your higher self (your soul) want you to know today?

What signs or symbols did you encounter or receive? What intuitive messages do you get through those signs or symbols you encountered?

Describe any people you encountered or circumstances that happened today that drained your energy:

How did you feel after this happened, what were your thoughts, and how was your body left feeling?

What spiritual cleansing, energetic cord cutting, energy healing, chakra clearing, visualization, mantra, prayer or meditation method did you use to clear the residual energy afterward from your body and auric field?

- [ ] Spiritual Cleansing
- [ ] Energy Healing
- [ ] Mantras
- [ ] Meditation
- [ ] Other
- [ ] Energetic Cord Cutting
- [ ] Chakra Clearing
- [ ] Visualization
- [ ] Prayers

What body sensations, intuitive thoughts or emotions did you feel today that helped you know you are going in the right direction for you?

What body sensations, intuitive thoughts or emotions did you feel today that helped you know you could be "off track" and need to take a step back?

What (pure) whole, nutritious foods did you eat that helped you feel better? Did you drink enough water?

what foods did you eat that caused you to feel worse?

How do you want tomorrow to be different?

what tiny (baby) steps would you like to take tomorrow for improved health, self-care, and that will move your life dreams and goals forward?

Circle or shade in how you feel today with one of the three face icons:

what are you most proud of about yourself for today?

Notes, brainstorming ideas or doodles:

Date   Day   Daily Intention

How did you feel when you first woke up this morning?

How did you feel in your dreams last night?

What intuitive messages does your higher self (your soul) want you to know today?

What signs or symbols did you encounter or receive? What intuitive messages do you get through those signs or symbols you encountered?

Describe any people you encountered or circumstances that happened today that drained your energy:

How did you feel after this happened, what were your thoughts, and how was your body left feeling?

What spiritual cleansing, energetic cord cutting, energy healing, chakra clearing, visualization, mantra, prayer or meditation method did you use to clear the residual energy afterward from your body and auric field?

- [ ] Spiritual Cleansing
- [ ] Energy Healing
- [ ] Mantras
- [ ] Meditation
- [ ] Other
- [ ] Energetic Cord Cutting
- [ ] Chakra Clearing
- [ ] Visualization
- [ ] Prayers

What body sensations, intuitive thoughts or emotions did you feel today that helped you know you are going in the right direction for you?

What body sensations, intuitive thoughts or emotions did you feel today that helped you know you could be "off track" and need to take a step back?

What (pure) whole, nutritious foods did you eat that helped you feel better? Did you drink enough water?

what foods did you eat that caused you to feel worse?

How do you want tomorrow to be different?

what tiny (baby) steps would you like to take tomorrow for improved health, self-care, and that will move your life dreams and goals forward?

Circle or shade in how you feel today with one of the three face icons:

What are you most proud of about yourself for today?

Notes, brainstorming ideas or doodles:

Date Day Daily Intention

How did you feel when you first woke up this morning?

How did you feel in your dreams last night?

What intuitive messages does your higher self (your soul) want you to know today?

What signs or symbols did you encounter or receive? What intuitive messages do you get through those signs or symbols you encountered?

Describe any people you encountered or circumstances that happened today that drained your energy:

How did you feel after this happened, what were your thoughts, and how was your body left feeling?

What spiritual cleansing, energetic cord cutting, energy healing, chakra clearing, visualization, mantra, prayer or meditation method did you use to clear the residual energy afterward from your body and auric field?

- [ ] Spiritual Cleansing
- [ ] Energy Healing
- [ ] Mantras
- [ ] Meditation
- [ ] Other
- [ ] Energetic Cord Cutting
- [ ] Chakra Clearing
- [ ] Visualization
- [ ] Prayers

What body sensations, intuitive thoughts or emotions did you feel today that helped you know you are going in the right direction for you?

What body sensations, intuitive thoughts or emotions did you feel today that helped you know you could be "off track" and need to take a step back?

What (pure) whole, nutritious foods did you eat that helped you feel better? Did you drink enough water?

What foods did you eat that caused you to feel worse?

How do you want tomorrow to be different?

What tiny (baby) steps would you like to take tomorrow for improved health, self-care, and that will move your life dreams and goals forward?

Circle or shade in how you feel today with one of the three face icons:

What are you most proud of about yourself for today?

Notes, brainstorming ideas or doodles:

Date _____   Day _____   Daily Intention _____

How did you feel when you first woke up this morning?

How did you feel in your dreams last night?

What intuitive messages does your higher self (your soul) want you to know today?

What signs or symbols did you encounter or receive? What intuitive messages do you get through those signs or symbols you encountered?

Describe any people you encountered or circumstances that happened today that drained your energy:

How did you feel after this happened, what were your thoughts, and how was your body left feeling?

What spiritual cleansing, energetic cord cutting, energy healing, chakra clearing, visualization, mantra, prayer or meditation method did you use to clear the residual energy afterward from your body and auric field?

- [ ] Spiritual Cleansing
- [ ] Energy Healing
- [ ] Mantras
- [ ] Meditation
- [ ] Other
- [ ] Energetic Cord Cutting
- [ ] Chakra Clearing
- [ ] Visualization
- [ ] Prayers

What body sensations, intuitive thoughts or emotions did you feel today that helped you know you are going in the right direction for you?

What body sensations, intuitive thoughts or emotions did you feel today that helped you know you could be "off track" and need to take a step back?

What (pure) whole, nutritious foods did you eat that helped you feel better? Did you drink enough water?

What foods did you eat that caused you to feel worse?

How do you want tomorrow to be different?

What tiny (baby) steps would you like to take tomorrow for improved health, self-care, and that will move your life dreams and goals forward?

Circle or shade in how you feel today with one of the three face icons:

What are you most proud of about yourself for today?

Notes, brainstorming ideas or doodles:

Date   Day   Daily Intention
_____   _____   _____

How did you feel when you first woke up this morning?

How did you feel in your dreams last night?

What intuitive messages does your higher self (your soul) want you to know today?

What signs or symbols did you encounter or receive? What intuitive messages do you get through those signs or symbols you encountered?

Describe any people you encountered or circumstances that happened today that drained your energy:

How did you feel after this happened, what were your thoughts, and how was your body left feeling?

What spiritual cleansing, energetic cord cutting, energy healing, chakra clearing, visualization, mantra, prayer or meditation method did you use to clear the residual energy afterward from your body and auric field?

- [ ] Spiritual Cleansing
- [ ] Energy Healing
- [ ] Mantras
- [ ] Meditation
- [ ] Other
- [ ] Energetic Cord Cutting
- [ ] Chakra Clearing
- [ ] Visualization
- [ ] Prayers

What body sensations, intuitive thoughts or emotions did you feel today that helped you know you are going in the right direction for you?

What body sensations, intuitive thoughts or emotions did you feel today that helped you know you could be "off track" and need to take a step back?

What (pure) whole, nutritious foods did you eat that helped you feel better? Did you drink enough water?

What foods did you eat that caused you to feel worse?

How do you want tomorrow to be different?

What tiny (baby) steps would you like to take tomorrow for improved health, self-care, and that will move your life dreams and goals forward?

Circle or shade in how you feel today with one of the three face icons:

What are you most proud of about yourself for today?

Notes, brainstorming ideas or doodles:

Date _____ Day _____ Daily Intention _____

How did you feel when you first woke up this morning?

How did you feel in your dreams last night?

What intuitive messages does your higher self (your soul) want you to know today?

What signs or symbols did you encounter or receive? What intuitive messages do you get through those signs or symbols you encountered?

Describe any people you encountered or circumstances that happened today that drained your energy:

How did you feel after this happened, what were your thoughts, and how was your body left feeling?

What spiritual cleansing, energetic cord cutting, energy healing, chakra clearing, visualization, mantra, prayer or meditation method did you use to clear the residual energy afterward from your body and auric field?

- [ ] Spiritual Cleansing
- [ ] Energy Healing
- [ ] Mantras
- [ ] Meditation
- [ ] Other
- [ ] Energetic Cord Cutting
- [ ] Chakra Clearing
- [ ] Visualization
- [ ] Prayers

What body sensations, intuitive thoughts or emotions did you feel today that helped you know you are going in the right direction for you?

What body sensations, intuitive thoughts or emotions did you feel today that helped you know you could be "off track" and need to take a step back?

What (pure) whole, nutritious foods did you eat that helped you feel better? Did you drink enough water?

what foods did you eat that caused you to feel worse?

How do you want tomorrow to be different?

what tiny (baby) steps would you like to take tomorrow for improved health, self-care, and that will move your life dreams and goals forward?

Circle or shade in how you feel today with one of the three face icons:

what are you most proud of about yourself for today?

Notes, brainstorming ideas or doodles:

Date _____ Day _____ Daily Intention _____

How did you feel when you first woke up this morning?

How did you feel in your dreams last night?

What intuitive messages does your higher self (your soul) want you to know today?

What signs or symbols did you encounter or receive? What intuitive messages do you get through those signs or symbols you encountered?

Describe any people you encountered or circumstances that happened today that drained your energy:

How did you feel after this happened, what were your thoughts, and how was your body left feeling?

What spiritual cleansing, energetic cord cutting, energy healing, chakra clearing, visualization, mantra, prayer or meditation method did you use to clear the residual energy afterward from your body and auric field?

- [ ] Spiritual Cleansing
- [ ] Energy Healing
- [ ] Mantras
- [ ] Meditation
- [ ] Other
- [ ] Energetic Cord Cutting
- [ ] Chakra Clearing
- [ ] Visualization
- [ ] Prayers

What body sensations, intuitive thoughts or emotions did you feel today that helped you know you are going in the right direction for you?

What body sensations, intuitive thoughts or emotions did you feel today that helped you know you could be "off track" and need to take a step back?

What (pure) whole, nutritious foods did you eat that helped you feel better? Did you drink enough water?

What foods did you eat that caused you to feel worse?

How do you want tomorrow to be different?

What tiny (baby) steps would you like to take tomorrow for improved health, self-care, and that will move your life dreams and goals forward?

Circle or shade in how you feel today with one of the three face icons:

What are you most proud of about yourself for today?

Notes, brainstorming ideas or doodles:

Date _____ Day _____ Daily Intention _____

How did you feel when you first woke up this morning?

How did you feel in your dreams last night?

What intuitive messages does your higher self (your soul) want you to know today?

What signs or symbols did you encounter or receive? What intuitive messages do you get through those signs or symbols you encountered?

Describe any people you encountered or circumstances that happened today that drained your energy:

How did you feel after this happened, what were your thoughts, and how was your body left feeling?

What spiritual cleansing, energetic cord cutting, energy healing, chakra clearing, visualization, mantra, prayer or meditation method did you use to clear the residual energy afterward from your body and auric field?

- [ ] Spiritual Cleansing
- [ ] Energy Healing
- [ ] Mantras
- [ ] Meditation
- [ ] Other
- [ ] Energetic Cord Cutting
- [ ] Chakra Clearing
- [ ] Visualization
- [ ] Prayers

What body sensations, intuitive thoughts or emotions did you feel today that helped you know you are going in the right direction for you?

What body sensations, intuitive thoughts or emotions did you feel today that helped you know you could be "off track" and need to take a step back?

What (pure) whole, nutritious foods did you eat that helped you feel better? Did you drink enough water?

what foods did you eat that caused you to feel worse?

How do you want tomorrow to be different?

what tiny (baby) steps would you like to take tomorrow for improved health, self-care, and that will move your life dreams and goals forward?

Circle or shade in how you feel today with one of the three face icons:

what are you most proud of about yourself for today?

Notes, brainstorming ideas or doodles:

Date _____   Day _____   Daily Intention _____

How did you feel when you first woke up this morning?

How did you feel in your dreams last night?

What intuitive messages does your higher self (your soul) want you to know today?

What signs or symbols did you encounter or receive? What intuitive messages do you get through those signs or symbols you encountered?

Describe any people you encountered or circumstances that happened today that drained your energy:

How did you feel after this happened, what were your thoughts, and how was your body left feeling?

What spiritual cleansing, energetic cord cutting, energy healing, chakra clearing, visualization, mantra, prayer or meditation method did you use to clear the residual energy afterward from your body and auric field?

- [ ] Spiritual Cleansing
- [ ] Energy Healing
- [ ] Mantras
- [ ] Meditation
- [ ] Other
- [ ] Energetic Cord Cutting
- [ ] Chakra Clearing
- [ ] Visualization
- [ ] Prayers

What body sensations, intuitive thoughts or emotions did you feel today that helped you know you are going in the right direction for you?

What body sensations, intuitive thoughts or emotions did you feel today that helped you know you could be "off track" and need to take a step back?

What (pure) whole, nutritious foods did you eat that helped you feel better? Did you drink enough water?

What foods did you eat that caused you to feel worse?

How do you want tomorrow to be different?

What tiny (baby) steps would you like to take tomorrow for improved health, self-care, and that will move your life dreams and goals forward?

Circle or shade in how you feel today with one of the three face icons:

What are you most proud of about yourself for today?

Notes, brainstorming ideas or doodles:

Date   Day   Daily Intention

How did you feel when you first woke up this morning?

How did you feel in your dreams last night?

What intuitive messages does your higher self (your soul) want you to know today?

What signs or symbols did you encounter or receive? What intuitive messages do you get through those signs or symbols you encountered?

Describe any people you encountered or circumstances that happened today that drained your energy:

How did you feel after this happened, what were your thoughts, and how was your body left feeling?

What spiritual cleansing, energetic cord cutting, energy healing, chakra clearing, visualization, mantra, prayer or meditation method did you use to clear the residual energy afterward from your body and auric field?

- [ ] Spiritual Cleansing
- [ ] Energy Healing
- [ ] Mantras
- [ ] Meditation
- [ ] Other
- [ ] Energetic Cord Cutting
- [ ] Chakra Clearing
- [ ] Visualization
- [ ] Prayers

What body sensations, intuitive thoughts or emotions did you feel today that helped you know you are going in the right direction for you?

What body sensations, intuitive thoughts or emotions did you feel today that helped you know you could be "off track" and need to take a step back?

What (pure) whole, nutritious foods did you eat that helped you feel better? Did you drink enough water?

what foods did you eat that caused you to feel worse?

How do you want tomorrow to be different?

what tiny (baby) steps would you like to take tomorrow for improved health, self-care, and that will move your life dreams and goals forward?

Circle or shade in how you feel today with one of the three face icons:

What are you most proud of about yourself for today?

Notes, brainstorming ideas or doodles:

Date _____   Day _____   Daily Intention _____

How did you feel when you first woke up this morning?

How did you feel in your dreams last night?

What intuitive messages does your higher self (your soul) want you to know today?

What signs or symbols did you encounter or receive? What intuitive messages do you get through those signs or symbols you encountered?

Describe any people you encountered or circumstances that happened today that drained your energy:

How did you feel after this happened, what were your thoughts, and how was your body left feeling?

What spiritual cleansing, energetic cord cutting, energy healing, chakra clearing, visualization, mantra, prayer or meditation method did you use to clear the residual energy afterward from your body and auric field?

- [ ] Spiritual Cleansing
- [ ] Energy Healing
- [ ] Mantras
- [ ] Meditation
- [ ] Other
- [ ] Energetic Cord Cutting
- [ ] Chakra Clearing
- [ ] Visualization
- [ ] Prayers

What body sensations, intuitive thoughts or emotions did you feel today that helped you know you are going in the right direction for you?

What body sensations, intuitive thoughts or emotions did you feel today that helped you know you could be "off track" and need to take a step back?

What (pure) whole, nutritious foods did you eat that helped you feel better? Did you drink enough water?

What foods did you eat that caused you to feel worse?

How do you want tomorrow to be different?

What tiny (baby) steps would you like to take tomorrow for improved health, self-care, and that will move your life dreams and goals forward?

Circle or shade in how you feel today with one of the three face icons:

What are you most proud of about yourself for today?

Notes, brainstorming ideas or doodles:

Date _____   Day _____   Daily Intention _____

How did you feel when you first woke up this morning?

How did you feel in your dreams last night?

What intuitive messages does your higher self (your soul) want you to know today?

What signs or symbols did you encounter or receive? What intuitive messages do you get through those signs or symbols you encountered?

Describe any people you encountered or circumstances that happened today that drained your energy:

How did you feel after this happened, what were your thoughts, and how was your body left feeling?

What spiritual cleansing, energetic cord cutting, energy healing, chakra clearing, visualization, mantra, prayer or meditation method did you use to clear the residual energy afterward from your body and auric field?

- [ ] Spiritual Cleansing
- [ ] Energy Healing
- [ ] Mantras
- [ ] Meditation
- [ ] Other
- [ ] Energetic Cord Cutting
- [ ] Chakra Clearing
- [ ] Visualization
- [ ] Prayers

What body sensations, intuitive thoughts or emotions did you feel today that helped you know you are going in the right direction for you?

What body sensations, intuitive thoughts or emotions did you feel today that helped you know you could be "off track" and need to take a step back?

What (pure) whole, nutritious foods did you eat that helped you feel better? Did you drink enough water?

What foods did you eat that caused you to feel worse?

How do you want tomorrow to be different?

What tiny (baby) steps would you like to take tomorrow for improved health, self-care, and that will move your life dreams and goals forward?

Circle or shade in how you feel today with one of the three face icons:

What are you most proud of about yourself for today?

Notes, brainstorming ideas or doodles:

Date	Day	Daily Intention
____	____	____

How did you feel when you first woke up this morning?

How did you feel in your dreams last night?

What intuitive messages does your higher self (your soul) want you to know today?

What signs or symbols did you encounter or receive? What intuitive messages do you get through those signs or symbols you encountered?

Describe any people you encountered or circumstances that happened today that drained your energy:

How did you feel after this happened, what were your thoughts, and how was your body left feeling?

What spiritual cleansing, energetic cord cutting, energy healing, chakra clearing, visualization, mantra, prayer or meditation method did you use to clear the residual energy afterward from your body and auric field?

- [ ] Spiritual Cleansing
- [ ] Energy Healing
- [ ] Mantras
- [ ] Meditation
- [ ] Other
- [ ] Energetic Cord Cutting
- [ ] Chakra Clearing
- [ ] Visualization
- [ ] Prayers

What body sensations, intuitive thoughts or emotions did you feel today that helped you know you are going in the right direction for you?

What body sensations, intuitive thoughts or emotions did you feel today that helped you know you could be "off track" and need to take a step back?

What (pure) whole, nutritious foods did you eat that helped you feel better? Did you drink enough water?

What foods did you eat that caused you to feel worse?

How do you want tomorrow to be different?

What tiny (baby) steps would you like to take tomorrow for improved health, self-care, and that will move your life dreams and goals forward?

Circle or shade in how you feel today with one of the three face icons:

What are you most proud of about yourself for today?

Notes, brainstorming ideas or doodles:

Date _____   Day _____   Daily Intention _____

How did you feel when you first woke up this morning?

How did you feel in your dreams last night?

What intuitive messages does your higher self (your soul) want you to know today?

What signs or symbols did you encounter or receive? What intuitive messages do you get through those signs or symbols you encountered?

Describe any people you encountered or circumstances that happened today that drained your energy:

How did you feel after this happened, what were your thoughts, and how was your body left feeling?

What spiritual cleansing, energetic cord cutting, energy healing, chakra clearing, visualization, mantra, prayer or meditation method did you use to clear the residual energy afterward from your body and auric field?

- [ ] Spiritual Cleansing
- [ ] Energy Healing
- [ ] Mantras
- [ ] Meditation
- [ ] Other
- [ ] Energetic Cord Cutting
- [ ] Chakra Clearing
- [ ] Visualization
- [ ] Prayers

What body sensations, intuitive thoughts or emotions did you feel today that helped you know you are going in the right direction for you?

What body sensations, intuitive thoughts or emotions did you feel today that helped you know you could be "off track" and need to take a step back?

What (pure) whole, nutritious foods did you eat that helped you feel better? Did you drink enough water?

What foods did you eat that caused you to feel worse?

How do you want tomorrow to be different?

What tiny (baby) steps would you like to take tomorrow for improved health, self-care, and that will move your life dreams and goals forward?

Circle or shade in how you feel today with one of the three face icons:

What are you most proud of about yourself for today?

Notes, brainstorming ideas or doodles:

Recommended Resources for Empaths...

9 FREE Archangel Michael Prayers of Protection PDF

FREE Anxiety Relief Archangel Michael Meditation

Archangel Michael House Clearing & Blessing Audio

Spiritual Cleansing (Empath Protection) Healing Sessions

Spiritual Cleansing (Empath Protection) Crystal Lights

Archangel Michael Protection Necklace (Blessed)

Mother Mary Protection Necklace (Blessed)

You can find all of the resources mentioned above at:

ArchangelsBless.com

One Last Thing...

If you enjoyed this journal or found it useful, I'd be very grateful if you'd post a short review on Amazon. Your support does make a difference, and I read all the reviews personally so I can get your feedback and make this journal even better.

Thanks again for leaving a quick review!

Made in the USA
Monee, IL
17 June 2021